junior knits

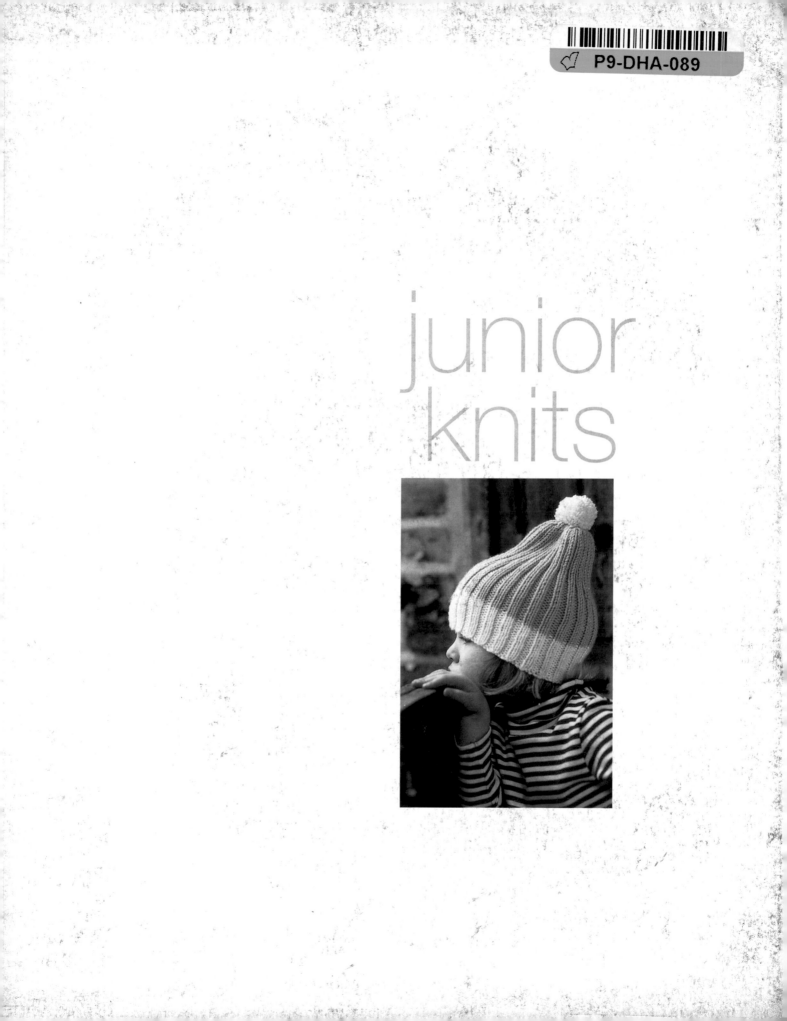

junior knits

25 stylish projects for children
three to ten years

Debbie Bliss

Trafalgar Square Publishing

Dedication:

For family, friends, and neighbors (particularly the Folkestone Road Dining Club)

First published in the United States of America in 2004 by
Trafalgar Square Publishing, North Pomfret, Vermont 05053

Printed and bound in Malaysia by Tien Wah Press

1 3 5 7 9 10 8 6 4 2

Text © Debbie Bliss 2004
Photographs © Sandra Lousada 2004

First published by Ebury Press
Random House, 20 Vauxhall Bridge Road, London SW1V 2SA

Editor: Emma Callery
Designer: Christine Wood
Photographer: Sandra Lousada
Stylist: Julie Mansfield
Pattern checker: Rosy Tucker

ISBN 1 57076 300 3

Library of Congress Control Number: 2004100378

Papers used by Ebury Press are natural, recyclable products made from wood grown in sustainable forests.

contents

Introduction 6

Knitting essentials 8

introduction

Junior Knits is a collection of 25 hand knits for toddlers to teens. Older children can sometimes be overlooked when it comes to design and it has been a fresh challenge to create a range of hand knits that I feel will appeal to a wider age range of children. Also, with so many new knitters around, I have designed some of them, such as Woody and Nell, to be quick and easy to knit, perfect for a beginner who will appreciate a sweater completed before the enthusiasm flags! The cover jacket (Mia) is knitted all-in-one, to eliminate some of the seams that the less experienced knitter may prefer not to tackle in the early stages, such as the armhole and shoulder seams. All the accessories are simple and the garter stitch scarf with pompons (Hattie) makes a great first project for a child to knit. For those who would like to achieve color without having to know complicated techniques, there are simple stripes in a hooded top (Bill) and hand and leg warmers (Cozy); while for knitters who like more of a challenge, there is a multi-patterned poncho (Ruby) that can be worn as a skirt or body warmer. There are sporty knits with hoods and zippers, and more feminine designs tied with ribbon or edged with a ruffle in soft cashmere mixes.

All the designs are knitted in my own brand of yarns, which have been chosen not just for their child-friendly handle but also for their easy wash and wear. The merino wools are gentle on the skin but stand up to tough wear and tear, the cashmere mixes add a touch of luxury to the designs, and for those who prefer to wear or knit in cotton, there is a soft double knitting yarn.

Children sometimes need to be persuaded into wearing hand-knitted garments. They might like the color or the design but are used to the lightweight feel of fleeces and sweatshirts, which also allow for plenty of movement. With this in mind I allow plenty of ease in my designs. Ease is the extra measurement allowed for comfort and movement that all garments have unless they are form-fitting adult pieces. In the past, readers have sometimes queried the quoted measurements on my children's designs because they are comparing an adult's chest measurements with the actual measurements of a child's garment. I usually ask them to measure an existing garment that the child they are knitting for wears and they are often surprised to find that they match closely with the ones I have suggested. I also feel that a knit should see a child through more than one season, even if this means the garment is

larger initially than is strictly needed. If the reader is not happy with the measurements, it is easy to check the actual sizes quoted and then knit a smaller size.

It can be a rewarding experience to involve the child in the garment that is being knitted for them. The choice of color is such an individual one, but be prepared for disappointment if the tasteful shade you may have chosen is rejected in favor of a scary fluorescent pink! You may be starting to encourage a lifelong passion for knitting.

knitting essentials

following pattern instructions

Figures for larger sizes are given in parentheses ( ). Where only one figure appears, this applies to all sizes. Work the figures given in brackets [ ] the number of times stated afterward. Where 0 appears, no stitches or rows are worked for this size. As you follow the pattern, make sure that you are consistently using the right stitches for your size; it is only too easy to switch sizes inside the brackets. One way to avoid this is to go through the instructions first and mark the figures for the size you are knitting with a colored marker or highlighter.

The quantities of yarn quoted in the instructions are based on the yarn used by the knitter for the original garment, and amounts should therefore be considered approximate. A slight variation in gauge can make the difference between using less or more yarn than that stated in the pattern. Before buying the yarn, look at the measurements in the knitting patterns to be sure which size you want to knit. My patterns quote the actual finished size of the garment, not the chest size of the wearer. The length of the garment is taken from the shoulder shaping to the cast-on edge.

gauge

Each pattern in the book states a gauge—the number of stitches and rows per inch that should be obtained with the given needles, yarn, and stitch pattern. Check your gauge carefully before starting work. A slight variation in gauge can spoil the look of a garment and alter the proportions that the designer wanted. A too loose gauge will produce uneven knitting and an unstable fabric that can droop or lose its shape after washing, while too tight a gauge can create a hard, unforgiving fabric.

To make a gauge square, use the same needles, yarn, and stitch pattern quoted in the gauge note in the pattern. Knit a sample at least 5in/12.5cm square. Smooth out the finished sample on a flat surface but do not stretch it. To check the stitch gauge, place a tape measure horizontally on the sample and mark 4in/10cm with pins. Count the number of stitches between pins. To check the row gauge, place the tape measure vertically on the sample and mark 4in/10cm. Count the number of rows between the pins. If the number of stitches and rows is greater than that stated in the pattern, try again using larger needles. If the number of stitches and rows is less, use smaller needles. If you are only able to obtain either the stitch or the row gauge, it is the stitch gauge that is the most important to get right, as the length of many patterns are calculated by measurement rather than the number of rows you need to work to achieve it.

garment care

Taking care of your knitted garments is important. If you have invested all that time and labor into knitting them, you want them to look good for as long as possible. Follow these guidelines for the best results.

Check the yarn label for washing instructions. Most yarns can now be machine-washed on a delicate wool cycle. Prior to washing, make a note of the measurements of the garment, such as the width and length. After washing, lay the garment flat and check the measurements again to see if they are the same. If not, smooth and pat it back into shape.

Some knitters prefer to hand wash their garments. Use laundry detergent specially created for hand knits, and warm rather than hot water. Handle the knits gently in the water; do not rub or wring, as this can felt the fabric. Rinse well to get rid of any soap, and squeeze out excess water. You may need to get rid of more water by rolling the garment in a towel, or you can use the delicate spin cycle of the washing machine. To dry the garment, lay it out flat on top of a towel, and smooth and pat it into shape. Do not dry knits near direct heat, such as a radiator. Store your knits loosely folded to allow the air to circulate.

needle conversion chart

This needle conversion chart covers all the knitting needle sizes used for the patterns in this book.

U.S. sizes	U.K. metric	U.S. sizes	U.K. metric
size 2	2¾mm	size 6	4mm
	3mm	size 7	4½mm
size 3	3¼mm	size 8	5mm
size 5	3¾mm	size 11	7½mm

knitting abbreviations

alt = alternate
beg = beginning
cm = centimeters
cont = continue
dec = decreas(e)ing
foll = following
g = grams
in = inches
inc = increas(e)ing
k = knit
kfb = k into front and back of st
kp = knit and purl into next st
m = meters
M1 = make one by

picking up loop lying between st just worked and next st and working into the back of it
oz = ounces
p = purl
patt = pattern
pk = purl and knit into next st
psso = pass slipped st over
rem = remain(ing)
rep = repeat
skp = slip 1, knit 1, pass slipped stitch over
sl = slip

ssk = [slip 1 knitwise] twice, insert tip of left needle into fronts of slipped sts and work 2 tog
St st = stockinette st
st(s) = stitch(es)
tbl = through back of loop
tog = together
yb = yarn to back of work
yd = yards
yf = yarn to front of work
yo = yarn over

types of yarns

wool

Wool spun from the fleece of sheep is the yarn that is the most commonly associated with knitting. It has many excellent qualities, as it is durable, elastic, and warm in the winter. Wool yarn is particularly good for working colorwork patterns, as the fibers adhere together and help prevent the gaps that can appear in Fair Isle or intarsia knitting.

Some knitters find that a simple stitch such as seed stitch or garter stitch can look neater when worked in a wool rather than a cotton yarn.

cotton

Cotton yarn, made from a natural plant fiber, is an ideal all-seasons yarn, as it is warm in the winter and cool in the summer. I particularly love to work in cotton because it gives a clarity of stitch that shows up subtle stitch patterning, such as a seed stitch border on a collar or cuffs.

cotton and wool

Knitting in yarn that is a blend of wool and cotton is particularly good for children's wear. The wool fibers give elasticity for comfort and the cotton content is perfect for children who find wool irritating against the skin.

cashmere

Cashmere is made from the underhair of a particular Asian goat. It is associated with the ultimate in luxury, and is unbelievably soft to the touch. If combined with merino wool and microfiber, as in my cashmerino yarn range, it is perfect for babies and children as well as adults.

buying yarn

Always try to buy the yarn quoted in the knitting pattern. The designer will have created the design specifically with that yarn in mind, and a substitute may produce a garment that is different from the original. For instance, the design may rely for its appeal on a subtle stitch pattern that is lost when using a yarn of an inferior quality; or a synthetic when used to replace a natural yarn such as cotton will create a limp fabric and the crispness of the original design will be lost. We cannot accept responsibility for the finished product if any yarn other than the one specified is used.

substituting yarn

If you do decide to use a substitute yarn, buy one that is the same weight and, if possible, has the same fiber content. It is essential to use a yarn that has the same gauge as the original or the measurements will change. Also check the yardage; yarn that weighs the same may have different lengths so you may need to buy more or less yarn. Most yarn labels now carry all the information you need about fiber content, washing instructions, weight, and yardage.

It is essential to check the dye lot number on the yarn label. Yarns are dyed in batches or lots, which can sometimes vary quite considerably. Your retailer may not have the same dye lot later on, so try to buy all your yarn for a project at the same time. If you know that sometimes you use more yarn than that quoted in the pattern, buy more. If it is not possible to buy the amount you need all in the same dye lot, work the borders or the lower edges in the odd one since the color change is less likely to show here.

Debbie Bliss yarns

The following are descriptions of my yarns and a guide to their weights and types. All the yarns used in the designs are machine washable. (See page 128 for yarn suppliers.)

Debbie Bliss merino double knitting—a 100% merino wool in a double-knitting weight. Soft to the touch but hardwearing. Approximately 120yd/1¾oz (110m/50g) ball.

Debbie Bliss merino aran—a 100% merino wool in an Aran weight. Ideal for outerwear. Approximately 85yd/1¾oz (78m/50g) ball.

Debbie Bliss cashmerino aran—a 55% merino wool, 33% microfiber, 12% cashmere yarn in an Aran weight. A luxurious yarn with a beautiful handle. Approximately 98yd/1¾oz (90m/50g) ball.

Debbie Bliss baby cashmerino—a 55% merino wool, 33% microfiber, 12% cashmere lightweight yarn between a sport and a double-knitting weight. It is perfect for knitting for newborn and small babies, as it is gentle against the skin. Approximately 91yd/1¾oz (84m/50g) ball.

Debbie Bliss cotton cashmere—an 85% cotton,15% cashmere yarn in a double-knitting weight. Soft but still has the crispness of cotton. Approximately 103yd/1¾oz (95m/50g) ball.

Debbie Bliss cotton denim aran—knits to an Aran weight. A soft and light, non-shrinking denim-look yarn. Approximately 74yd/1¾oz (68m/50g) ball.

Debbie Bliss aran tweed—a 100% wool in an Aran weight. A classic tweed with bright flecks. Approximately 100yd/1¾oz (92m/50g) ball.

Nell

This raglan-sleeved sweater has been knitted in my cashmerino aran, a cashmere mix, to add a touch of luxury to a simple sweater. The back and front are the same so there is no complicated neck shaping. The mittens can button on to prevent them from escaping.

measurements

Sweater	to fit	3–4	5–6	7–8	9–10	years
Actual measurements						
Chest		30¾	34¼	38	41½	in
		78	87	96	105	cm
Length		14¼	15¾	17¼	19¾	in
		36	40	44	50	cm
Sleeve seam		10	11½	13½	15¾	in
		26	29	34	40	cm

Mittens	to fit	3–5	6–8 years

materials

Sweater 5(6:7:8) 1¾oz/50g balls of Debbie Bliss cashmerino aran in Lilac

Mittens One 1¾oz/50g ball of Debbie Bliss cashmerino aran in Lilac
Pair each size 7 and 8 (U.K. 4½mm and 5mm) knitting needles
4 small buttons for mittens

gauge

18 sts and 24 rows to 4in/10cm square over St st using size 8 (5mm) needles.

abbreviations

beg = beginning
cont = continue
cm = centimeters
foll = following
in = inches
inc = increase(e)ing
k = knit
M1 = make one st by picking up and working into back of loop lying between sts

p = purl
psso = pass slipped st over
rem = remain(ing)
rep = repeat
skp = slip 1, knit 1, pass slipped stitch over
sl = slip
ssk = (slip 1 knitwise) twice, insert tip of left

needle into fronts of slipped sts and work 2 tog
st(s) = stitch(es)
St st = stockinette stitch
tbl = through back of loop
tog = together
yo = yarn over

sweater

back and front

(both alike)

With size 7 (4½mm) needles, cast on 72(80:88:96) sts.

K 2 rows.

Change to size 8 (5mm) needles.

Beg with a k row, work in St st until back/front measures 7½(8¾:10¾:11¾)in/19(22:27:30)cm, ending with a p row.

** **Shape raglans**

Bind off 3(3:5:5) sts at beg of next 2 rows.

Next row (right side) K3, skp, k to last 5 sts, k2tog, k3.

Next row P. **

Rep the last 2 rows until 24(28:28:32) sts rem, ending with a p row.

Leave these sts on a holder.

sleeves

With size 7 (4½mm) needles, cast on 40(42:46:46) sts.

K 2 rows.

Change to size 8 (5mm) needles.

Beg with a k row, work 2(4:4:2) rows in St st.

Next row (right side) K3, M1, k to last 3 sts, M1, k3.

Cont in St st and inc as before on every foll 6th row until there are

60(64:72:76) sts.

Work even until sleeve measures 10(11½:13½:15¾)in/26(29:34:40)cm from cast-on edge, ending with a p row.

Now work exactly as for Back and Front from ** to **.

Rep the last 2 rows until 12 sts rem, ending with a p row.

Leave these sts on a holder.

neckband

Join three raglan seams, leaving left back raglan open.

With right side facing and size 7 (4½mm) needles, k first 11 sts from left sleeve holder, then k last st of sleeve tog with first st of front, k to last st of front, k last st tog with first st of right sleeve, k to last st of sleeve, k last st tog with first st of back, k to end. 69(77:77:85) sts.

Beg with a p row, work 12 rows in St st.

K 2 rows.

Bind off knitwise.

finishing

Join raglan and neckband seam. Join side and sleeve seams.

mittens

left mitten

With size 7 (4½mm) needles, cast on 30(36) sts.

Buttonhole row (right side) K16(21), k2tog tbl, yo, k7(8), yo, k2tog, k3.

K 1 row.

Beg with a k row, work 10(14) rows in St st.

Shape thumb

1st row (right side) K12(14), M1, k2, M1, k16(20). P 1 row.

3rd row K12(14), M1, k4, M1, k16(20). P 1 row.

5th row K12(14), M1, k6, M1, k16(20). P 1 row.

7th row (right side) K20(22), turn, cast on one st, p9, turn, cast on one st, k10.

*** Work a further 7(9) rows in St st on these 10 sts only for thumb.

Next row (right side) [K2tog] to end. 5 sts.

Break yarn, thread through rem sts, draw up, and secure. Join thumb seam. With right side facing, rejoin yarn to base of thumb, pick up 3 sts at base of thumb and k to end, so completing 7th row. 31(37) sts.

Beg with a p row, work 9(11) rows in St st.

Shape top

Next row K1, k2tog, k10(13), k2tog tbl, k1, k2tog, k10(13), k2tog tbl, k1.

Work 3 rows.

Next row K1, k2tog, k8(11), k2tog tbl, k1, k2tog, k8(11), k2tog tbl, k1.

P 1 row.

Next row K1, k2tog, k6(9), k2tog tbl, k1, k2tog, k6(9), k2tog tbl, k1.

P 1 row.

Next row K1, k2tog, k4(7), k2tog tbl, k1, k2tog, k4(7), k2tog tbl, k1.

2nd size only

P 1 row.

Next row K1, k2tog, k5, k2tog tbl, k1, k2tog, k5, k2tog tbl, k1.

Both sizes

Bind off rem 15(17) sts.

Join top and side seam.

right mitten

With size 7 (4½mm) needles, cast on 30(36) sts.

Buttonhole row (right side) K3, k2tog tbl, yo, k7(8), yo, k2tog, k16(21).

K 1 row.

Beg with a k row, work 10(14) rows in St st.

Shape thumb

1st row (right side) K16(20), M1, k2, M1, k12(14). P 1 row.

3rd row K16(20), M1, k4, M1, k12(14). P 1 row.

5th row K16(20), M1, k6, M1, k12(14). P 1 row.

7th row (right side) K24(28), turn, cast on one st, p9, turn, cast on one st, k10.

Now work exactly as given for Left Mitten from *** to end.

Woody

This sweater is a perfect beginner's knit worked in simple stockinette stitch with garter stitch edgings. For the neckband, you just pick up and knit one row. The shoulder seams are created on the outside to form a ridge detail similar to that in a traditional Guernsey.

measurements	**To fit ages**	3–4	5–6	7–8	9–10	years
	Actual measurements					
	Chest	33	36	37½	41	in
		84	91	95	104	cm
	Length	18	19¼	21	22½	in
		46	49	53	57	cm
	Sleeve seam	12	12½	14½	15¾	in
		30	32	37	40	cm

materials

8(9:11:12) 1¾oz/50g balls Debbie Bliss merino aran in Grey
Pair each size 7 and 8 (U.K. 4½mm and 5mm) knitting needles

gauge

18 sts and 24 rows to 4in/10cm square over St st using size 8 (5mm) needles.

abbreviations

beg = beginning
cm = centimeters
cont = continue
dec = decreas(e)ing
foll = following

in = inches
inc = increas(e)ing
k = knit
p = purl

rem = remain(ing)
St st = stockinette stitch
st(s) = stitch(es)
tog = together

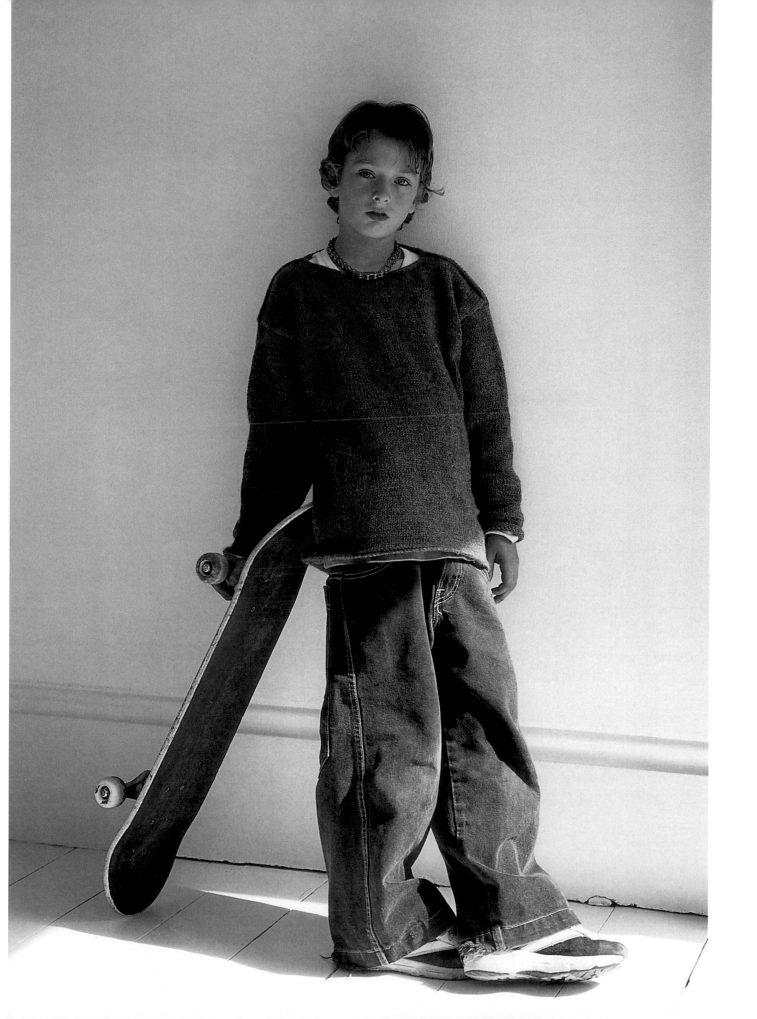

sweater

back

With size 7 (4½mm) needles, cast on 76(82:86:94) sts.
K 2 rows.
Change to size 8 (5mm) needles.
Beg with a k row, work in St st until back measures 10¼(10¾:11½:12¼)in/ 26(27:29:31)cm from cast-on edge, ending with a p row.
Shape armholes
Bind off 4(4:5:5) sts at beg of next 2 rows. 68(74:76:84) sts. **
Work even in St st until back measures 18(19¼:21:22½)in/46(49:53:57)cm from cast-on edge, ending with a p row.
Leave all sts on a spare needle for shoulders and back neck.

front

Work as given for Back to **, then work even in St st until front is 12(12:14:14) rows less than Back, so ending with a p row.
Shape neck
Next row (right side) K29(31:31:34) sts, turn.
Work on this set of sts only and dec one st at neck edge on every row until 20(22:22:25) sts rem.
Work a further 2(2:4:4) rows even.
Leave sts on a spare needle.
With right side facing, slip center 10(12:14:16) sts onto a holder, rejoin yarn to rem sts and k to end.
P 1 row.
Complete to match first side.

sleeves

With size 7 (4½mm) needles, cast on 32(34:36:36) sts.

K 2 rows.

Change to size 8 (5mm) needles.

Beg with a k row, work in St st and inc one st at each end of 7th and every foll 4th row until there are 64(68:74:78) sts.

Work even until sleeve measures 12(12½:14½:15¾)in/30(32:37:40)cm from cast-on edge, ending with a p row.

Mark each end of last row with colored thread, then work a further 6(6:8:8) rows.

Bind off.

neckband

Place 20(22:22:25) sts of Right Back shoulder on a separate needle. With wrong sides of Back and Front together and right side of front facing, k tog right shoulder sts and bind off.

With right side facing and size 7 (4½mm) needles, pick up and k 14(14:16:16) sts down left front neck, k across 10(12:14:16) sts at center front, pick up and k 14(14:16:16) sts up right front neck, then k 28(30:32:34) sts at back neck. 66(70:78:82) sts.

K 1 row. Bind off.

finishing

Join left shoulder seam in same way as right shoulder seam, then join neckband seam. Sew sleeves into armholes, with row ends above markers sewn to bound-off sts at underarm. Join side and sleeve seams.

Daisy

This bag is knitted in seed stitch and enlivened with a stockinette-stitch lining in a contrasting bright shade for a flash of color. The flowers are easy to create by working turning rows.

size

Approximately 8¾in x 7in/22cm x 18cm.

materials

Two 1¾oz/50g balls Debbie Bliss merino aran in each of Apple Green (A) and Bright Pink (B)
One 1¾oz/50g ball Debbie Bliss merino dk in Claret (C)
Pair each size 3, 6, and 7 (U.K. 3¼mm, 4mm, and 4½mm) knitting needles

gauges

20 sts and 34 rows to 4in/10cm square over seed st using size 7 (4½mm) needles and 22 sts and 30 rows to 4in/10cm square over St st using size 6 (4mm) needles, both with merino aran.

abbreviations

beg = beginning
cont = continue
cm = centimeters
in = inches

k = knit
kfb = knit into front and back of next st
p = purl

sl = slip
st(s) = stitch(es)
St st = stockinette stitch

bag

to make

Inner bag

With size 6 (4mm) needles and B, cast on 45 sts.

Beg with a k row, work in St st for 6¼in/16cm, ending with a p row.

Next row K15, bind off next 15 sts, k to end.

Next row P and cast on 15 sts over bound-off sts of previous row.

Work 5 rows more.

Next row (wrong side) K.

Outer bag

Change to size 7 (4½mm) needles and A.

K 1 row.

Seed st row K1, [p1, k1] to end.

Work 3 rows more in seed st.

Shape handle

Next row Seed st 15, bind off next 15 sts, seed st to end.

Next row Seed st and cast on 15 sts over bound-off sts of previous row.

Cont in seed st for a further 110 rows.

Next row (right side) Seed st 15, bind off next 15 sts, seed st to end.

Next row Seed st and cast on 15 sts over bound-off sts of previous row.

Work 4 rows in seed st.

Inner bag

Change to size 6 (4mm) needles and B.

K 2 rows.

Beg with a k row, work 4 rows in St st.

Next row K15, bind off next 15 sts, k to end.

Next row P and cast on 15 sts over bound-off sts of previous row.

Work a further 6¼in/16cm in St st, ending with a p row.

Bind off.

finishing

Join cast-on and bound-off edges to form base of inner bag. Join side seams of inner bag and side seams of outer bag. Slip stitch inner bag to outer bag around handle openings.

daisies (make 6)

With 3¼mm (US 3) needles and C, cast on 4 sts.

First petal

* **1st pair of rows** Kfb, k1, turn, sl 1, k2. 5 sts.

Next row Kfb, k to end. 6 sts.

Next row K.

2nd pair of rows Kfb, k3, turn, sl 1, k to end. 7 sts. **

Next row Cast off 3, k to end. 4 sts.

Next row K. ***

2nd, 3rd and 4th petals

Rep from * to *** 3 times more.

5th petal

Work from * to ** of first petal.

Next row Cast off all sts.

Join cast-on edge to last 4 sts of bound-off edge to form flower.

Attach three daisies each to front and back of bag with a large French knot worked in A in the center of each flower.

Rae

A grown-up, classic jacket in simple yet stylish seed stitch. Knitted in a brightly colored tweed yarn, it is trimmed with a frilled ribbon.

measurements

To fit ages	3–4	5–7	8–9	9–10	years
Actual measurements					
Chest	29¼	31½	33¾	35½	in
	74	80	86	90	cm
Length to shoulder	14	15¾	17	18	in
	36	40	43	46	cm
Sleeve length	10	11	13	15	in
	25	28	33	38	cm

materials

6(7:8:9) 1¾oz/50g balls of Debbie Bliss aran tweed in Fuchsia
Pair of size 8 (U.K. 5mm) knitting needles
1⅝(1¾:1⅞:2)yd/1.5(1.6:1.7:1.8)m double frilled edge ribbon

gauge

18 sts and 29 rows to 4in/10cm square over seed st using size 8 (5mm) needles.

abbreviations

alt = alternate
beg = beginning
cont = continue
cm = centimeters
dec = decreas(e)ing

foll = following
in = inches
inc = increas(e)ing
k = knit

p = purl
rem = remain(ing)
rep = repeat
st(s) = stitch(es)

jacket

back

With size 8 (5mm) needles, cast on 69(75:79:85) sts.

Seed st row K1, [p1, k1] to end.

Rep the last row until Back measures 8¼(9½:10¼:11)in/21(24:26:28)cm from cast-on edge, ending with a wrong side row.

Shape armholes

Bind off 5(6:7:8) sts at beg of next 2 rows. 59(63:65:69) sts.

Work even until Back measures 14¼(15¾:17:18)in/36(40:43:46)cm from cast-on edge, ending with a wrong side row.

Shape shoulders

Bind off 8(9:9:10) sts at beg of next 2 rows and 9(9:10:10) sts at beg of foll 2 rows.

Bind off rem 25(27:27:29) sts.

left front

With size 8 (5mm) needles, cast on 35(37:39:43) sts.

Seed st row K1, [p1, k1] to end.

Rep the last row until Front measures 8¼(9½:10¼:11)in/21(24:26:28)cm from cast-on edge, ending with a wrong side row.

Shape armholes

Bind off 5(6:7:8) sts at beg of next row. 30(31:32:35) sts.

Cont in seed st until Front measures 12(13½:14¼:15)in/31(34:36:38)cm from cast-on edge, ending at front edge.

Shape neck

Bind off 7(8:9:10) sts at beg of next row.

Dec one st at neck edge on every foll alt row until 17(18:19:20) sts rem.

Work even until Front matches Back to shoulder shaping, ending at armhole edge.

Shape shoulders

Bind off 8(9:9:10) sts at beg of next row.

Work 1 row.

Bind off rem 9(9:10:10) sts.

right front Work as Left Front, reversing all shapings.

sleeves

First half
With size 8 (5mm) needles, cast on 17(17:19:19) sts.
Seed st row K1, [p1, k1] to end.
Rep the last row 13 times more.
Leave the sts on a holder.

Second half
With size 8 (5mm) needles, cast on 17(17:19:19) sts.
Seed st row P1, [k1, p1] to end.
Rep the last row 13 times more.
Joining row (right side) [K1, p1] into first st, then work in seed st as set across rem 16(16:18:18) sts of second half and all sts of first half. 35(35:39:39) sts.
Cont in seed st, inc one st at each end of the 3rd and every foll 6th row until there are 53(57:63:67) sts.
Work even until sleeve measures 9¾(11:13:15)in/25(28:33:38)cm from cast-on edge, ending with a wrong side row.
Mark each end of last row, then work a further 8(9:11:12) rows.
Bind off.

finishing Join shoulder seams. Matching center of bound-off edge of sleeve to shoulder, sew sleeves into armholes with row ends above markers sewn to bound-off sts at underarm. Join side and sleeve seams. Fold ribbon in half lengthwise and stitch around the front and neck edges, stitching through the folded edge with the frilled edges facing away from the garment. Stitch ribbon around lower sleeve edges in the same way.

Jay

This is a really simple sweater made in my denim yarn, which has been created to give a faded look but without having dye loss or shrinkage. A contrasting band inside the opening gives a flash of color and hides the zipper edges.

measurements	To fit ages	2–3	4–5	6–7	years
	Actual measurements				
	Chest	32¼	35¾	38¼	in
		82	91	97	cm
	Length	17	18	20½	in
		43	46	52	cm
	Sleeve length	12½	13¾	15¾	in
		32	35	40	cm

materials

8(9:10) 1¾oz/50g balls of Debbie Bliss cotton denim aran in Medium Blue
Small amount cashmerino aran or merino aran in a contrasting shade for front opening edging
Pair each size 6 and 7 (U.K. 4mm and 4½mm) needles
Short size 6 (4mm) circular needle
4in/10cm zipper

gauge

18 sts and 24 rows to 4in/10cm square over St st using size 7 (4½mm) needles.

abbreviations

beg = beginning	**in** = inches	**rem** = remain(ing)
cm = centimeters	**inc** = increas(e)ing	**rep** = repeat
cont = continue	**k** = knit	**st(s)** = stitch(es)
dec = decreas(e)ing	**p** = purl	**St st** = stockinette stitch
foll = following		

sweater

back

With size 6 (4mm) needles, cast on 76(84:90) sts.
K 3 rows.
Change to size 7 (4½mm) needles.
Next row (right side) K to end.
Next row K3, p to last 3 sts, k3.
Rep the last 2 rows once more.
Beg with a k row, work in St st until back measures 11(11¾:13)in/28(30:33)cm from cast-on edge, ending with a wrong side row.
Shape armholes
Bind off 5(6:7) sts at beg of next 2 rows. ** 66(72:76) sts.
Work even until Back measures 17(18:20½)in/43(46:52)cm from cast-on edge, ending with a wrong side row.
Shape shoulders
Bind off 9(10:10) sts at beg of next 2 rows and 9(10:11) sts at beg of foll 2 rows.
Leave rem 30(32:34) sts on a holder.

front

Work as given for Back to **.
Divide for front opening
Next row (right side) K33(36:38), turn and work on these sts only.
Next row K2, p to end.
Next row K to end.
Next row K2, p to end.
Rep the last 2 rows ten times more.
Shape neck
Next row (right side) K to last 10 sts, turn, leave rem sts on a holder.
Dec one st at neck edge on next 5(6:7) rows.
Work even until Front measures the same as Back to shoulder, ending at armhole edge.
Shape shoulder
Bind off 9(10:10) sts at beg of next row.
Work 1 row.
Bind off rem 9(10:11) sts.
With right side facing, rejoin yarn to rem sts at center front, k to end.
Next row P to last 2 sts, k2.
Next row K to end.

Next row P to last 2 sts, k2.

Rep the last 2 rows ten times more.

Shape neck

Next row (right side) K10 sts, leave these sts on a holder, k to end.

Dec one st at neck edge on next 5(6:7) rows.

Work even until Front measures the same as Back to shoulder, ending at armhole edge.

Shape shoulder

Bind off 9(10:10) sts at beg of next row.

Work 1 row.

Bind off rem 9(10:11) sts.

collar

Join shoulder seams.

With a size 6 (4mm) circular needle and right side facing, slip 10 sts from Right Front holder onto a needle, pick up and k 11(12:13) sts up right front, k across 30(32:34) sts at back neck, pick up and k 11(12:13) sts down left side of front neck, then k across sts from Left Front holder. 72(76:80) sts.

Working backward and forward in rows, work in garter st (k every row) until collar measures 2¼(2¾:3)in/6(7:8)cm.

Bind off.

sleeves

With size 6 (4mm) needles cast on 40(44:48) sts.

K 3 rows.

Change to size 7 (4½mm) needles.

Beg with a k row, work in St st and inc one st at each end of the 9th(5th:9th) and every foll 8th(8th:6th) row until there are 54(62:72) sts.

Work even until sleeve measures 12½(13¾:15¾)in/32(35:40)cm from cast-on edge, ending with a p row.

Mark each end of last row with a colored thread.

Work 4(6:6) more rows.

Bind off.

front opening

edging (make 2)

With size 6 (4mm) needles and cashmerino aran, cast on 3 sts.

Work in garter st until edging is 4¼in/11cm long.

Bind off.

finishing

Matching center of bound-off edge of sleeve to shoulder, sew sleeves into armholes with row ends above markers sewn to bound-off sts at underarm. Join sleeve and side seams to top of side slit. Sew in zipper. Sew garter st edging to inside of front opening, covering zipper tape.

Meg

A classic parka, all the details are here, from the fishtail back to the corded waist fastening and hood. The coat is knitted in a 100% cotton for a lightweight jacket.

measurements						
To fit ages	4–6	6–8	8–10	10–12	years
Actual measurements					
Length (front to shoulder)	20	20¾	22½	23	in
	51	53	57	59	cm
Sleeve	10¾	12½	13¾	15¾	in
	27	32	35	40	cm

materials

15(16:18:20) 1¾oz/50g balls of Debbie Bliss cotton dk in Stone
Pair each size 3 and 6 (U.K. 3¼mm and 4mm) knitting needles
Size 6 (4mm) circular needle
20(20:22:22)in/50(50:55:55)cm open-ended zipper
8 buttons

gauge

20 sts and 28 rows to 4in/10cm square over St st using size 6 (4mm) needles.

abbreviations

beg = beginning
cont = continue
cm = centimeters
dec = decreas(e)ing
foll = following
in = inches
inc = increas(e)ing
k = knit

kfb = k into front and back of st
p = purl
patt = pattern
skp = slip 1, knit 1, pass slipped stitch over
sl = slip
st(s) = stitch(es)

St st = stockinette stitch
tbl = through back of loop
tog = together
yb = yarn to back of work
yf = yarn to front of work
yo = yarn over

parka

notes

- All slip stitches are slipped purlwise.
- Check length of front opening on your parka before buying the zipper. If the zipper does not fit exactly and it is too short, position it slightly above the hemline. If it is too long, trim and secure ends at neck edge.

back

Left Back

With size 6 (4mm) needles, cast on 49(52:55:58) sts.

K 4 rows.

Shape fishtail

1st row (right side) K4, yf, sl1, yb, turn.

2nd row Sl1, yb, k4.

3rd row K6, yf, sl1, yb, turn.

4th row Sl1, p2, k4.

5th row K8, yf, sl1, yb, turn.

6th row Sl1, p4, k4.

7th row K12, yf, sl1, yb, turn.

8th row Sl1, p8, k4.

9th row K16, yf, sl1, yb, turn.

10th row Sl1, p12, k4.

11th row K20, yf, sl1, yb, turn.

12th row Sl1, p16, k4.

13th row K24, yf, sl1, yb, turn.

14th row Sl1, p20, k4.

15th row K28, yf, sl1, yb, turn.

16th row Sl1, p24, k4.

17th row K32, yf, sl1, yb, turn.

18th row Sl1, p28, k4.

19th row K36, yf, sl1, yb, turn.

20th row Sl1, p32, k4.

21st row K40, yf, sl1, yb, turn.

22nd row Sl1, p36, k4.

23rd row K44, yf, sl1, yb, turn.

24th row Sl1, p40, k4.

2nd, 3rd, and 4th sizes only

25th row K48, yf, sl1, yb, turn.

26th row Sl1, p44, k4.

3rd and 4th sizes only

27th row K52, yf, sl1, yb, turn.

28th row Sl1, p48, k4.

4th size only

29th row K56, yf, sl1, yb, turn.

30th row Sl1, p52, k4.

All sizes

Next row (right side) K to end. 49(52:55:58) sts.

Next row P to last 4 sts, k4.

The last 2 rows form St st with k4 back vent edging.

Buttonhole row (right side) K2, yo, k2tog, k to end.

Cont in St st with k4 vent edging, make 2nd buttonhole on foll 16th row.

Work 1 row.

Dec row (right side) K to last 4 sts, skp, k2.

Making two more buttonholes each 16 rows apart, **at the same time** dec in this way at end of 4 foll 8th(8th:10th:10th) rows. 44(47:50:53) sts.

Work 3(5:1:3) rows.

Leave sts on a holder.

Right Back

With size 6 (4mm) needles, cast on 49(52:55:58) sts.

K 5 rows.

Shape fishtail

1st row (wrong side) K4, yf, sl1, yb, turn.

2nd row Sl1, yb, k4.

3rd row K4, p2, sl1, yb, turn.

4th row Sl1, yb, k6.

5th row K4, p4, sl1, yb, turn.

6th row Sl1, yb, k8.

7th row K4, p8, sl1, yb, turn.

8th row Sl1, yb, k12.

9th row K4, p12, sl1, yb, turn.

10th row Sl1, yb, k16.

11th row K4, p16, sl1, yb, turn.

12th row Sl1, yb, k20.

13th row K4, p20, sl1, yb, turn.

14th row Sl1, yb, k24.

15th row K4, p24, sl1, yb, turn.

16th row Sl1, yb, k28.

17th row K4, p28, sl1, yb, turn.

18th row Sl1, yb, k32.
19th row K4, p32, sl1, yb, turn.
20th row Sl1, yb, k36.
21st row K4, p36, sl1, yb, turn.
22nd row Sl1, yb, k40.
23rd row K4, p40, sl1, yb, turn.
24th row Sl1, yb, k44.

2nd, 3rd, and 4th sizes only

25th row K4, p44, sl1, yb, turn.
26th row Sl1, yb, k48.

3rd and 4th sizes only

27th row K4, p48, sl1, yb, turn.
28th row Sl1, yb, k52.

4th size only

29th row K4, p52, sl1, yb, turn.
30th row Sl1, yb, k56.

All sizes

Next row (wrong side) K4, p to end. 49(52:55:58) sts.
Next row K.

The last 2 rows form St st with k4 back vent edging.

Work 17 more rows.

Dec row (right side) K2, k2tog, k to end.

Cont in St st with k4 vent edging, dec in this way at beg of 4 foll
8th(8th:10th:10th) rows. 44(47:50:53) sts.

Work 3(5:1:3) rows.

Joining row (right side) K 40(43:46:49) sts of Right Back, overlapping Left
Back in front of right back, k each st of left vent edging tog with
corresponding st of right vent edging, k 40(43:46:49) sts of left back.
84(90:96:102) sts.

Cord channel

Change to size 3 (3¼mm) needles.

1st row (wrong side) K.
2nd row K1, [yo, k1] to end.
3rd row Sl1, yb, [k1 tbl, yf, sl1, yb] to end
4th row [K1, yf, sl1, yb] to last st, k1.

The last 2 rows form double fabric.

Next 3 rows Rep 3rd, 4th, and 3rd rows again.
Next row (right side) K1, [k2tog] to last 2 sts, k2. 85(91:97:103) sts.
Next row (wrong side) K.

Change to size 6 (4mm) needles.

Beg with a k row, work 2 rows in St st.

Inc row (right side) K1, kfb, k to last 3 sts, kfb, k2. 87(93:99:105) sts.

Cont in St st, inc in this way at each end of 4 foll 8th rows. 95(101:107:113) sts.

Work 5(9:13:13) rows in St st.

Shape armholes

Bind off 5 sts at beg of next 2 rows. 85(91:97:103) sts.

Dec row (right side) K2, k2tog, k to last 4 sts, skp, k2.

Cont in St st, dec in this way at each end of next 6 right side rows. 71(77:83:89) sts.

Work 1(1:1:3) rows in St st.

Yoke

1st row P1, [k1, p1] to end.

2nd row K1, [p1, k1] to end.

3rd row K1, [p1, k1] to end.

4th row P1, [k1, p1] to end.

These 4 rows form seed st patt.

Patt 16(18:22:24) more rows. Bind off.

pocket linings

(make 2)

With size 6 (4mm) needles, cast on 21(23:25:27) sts.

Beg with a k row, work 28(30:32:34) rows in St st. Leave sts on a holder.

pocket tops

(make 2)

With size 6 (4mm) needles, cast on 21(23:25:27) sts.

K 2 rows.

Buttonhole row (right side) K3, yo, k2tog, k11(13:15:17), skp, yo, k3.

Next row (wrong side) K4, p13(15:17:19), k4.

Cont in St st with k4 at each side for edgings, work 8(8:10:10) more rows. Leave sts on a holder.

left front

With size 6 (4mm) needles, cast on 47(50:53:56) sts.

K 5 rows.

Next row (wrong side) K2, p to end.

Cont in St st with k2 front edging.

Work 10 rows more.

Pocket front

1st row (right side) K15(16:17:18), p1, [k1, p1] 10(11:12:13) times, k11.

2nd row K2, p9, [k1, p1] 10(11:12:13) times, k1, p15(16:17:18).

3rd row K16(17:18:19), [p1, k1] 9(10:11:12) times, p1, k12.

4th row K2, p10, [k1, p1] 9(10:11:12) times, k1, p16(17:18:19).

These 4 rows form seed st for pocket front with St st to each side and k2 front edging.

Work 4 rows more.

Dec row (right side) K2, k2tog, patt to end.

Cont in patt, dec in this way at beg of 2 foll 8th(8th:10th:10th) rows. 44(47:50:53) sts.

Work 2(4:2:4) rows.

Pocket opening row (wrong side) K2, p9, bind off 21(23:25:27) sts of pocket front knitwise, p to end.

Place pocket top and lining

Next row (right side) K12(13:14:15), with pocket top in front of pocket lining, k one st of top and one st of lining tog each time to make 21(23:25:27) sts, k11. 44(47:50:53) sts.

Cont in St st with k2 front edging, work 3(1:5:3) rows.

Dec at beg of next row and on foll 8th(8th:10th:10th) row. 42(45:48:51) sts.

Work 4(6:2:4) rows.

Cord channel

Change to size 3 (3¼mm) needles.

1st row (wrong side) K.

2nd row [K1, yo] to last 2 sts, taking care not to lose the last yo, turn.

3rd row [K1 tbl, yf, sl1, yb] to end.

4th row [K1, yf, sl1, yb] to last 2 sts, k2.

5th row K3, [yf, sl1, yb, k1] to last st, yf, sl1, yb.

6th row [K1, yf, sl1, yb] to last 2 sts, omitting last yb, turn.

7th row [K1, yf, sl1, yb] to end.

8th row K1, [k2tog] to last st, k1. 42(45:48:51) sts.

9th row K.

Change to size 6 (4mm) needles.

Beg with a k row, work 2 rows in St st with k2 at front edge.

Work 2 rows.

Inc row (right side) K1, kfb, k to end.

Cont in St st with k2 at front edge on every row, inc in this way at beg of 4 foll 8th rows. 47(50:53:56) sts.

Work 5(9:13:13) rows.

Shape armhole

Bind off 5 sts at beg of next row.

Work 1 row.

Dec row (right side) K2, k2tog, k to end.

Cont in St st with k2 at front edge, dec in this way at beg of next 6 right side rows. 35(38:41:44) sts.

Work 1(1:1:3) rows.

Yoke

1st row P1(0:1:0), [k1, p1] to last 2 sts, k2.

2nd row K3, [p1, k1] to last 0(1:0:1) st, p0(1:0:1).

3rd row P0(1:0:1), [k1, p1] to last 3 sts, k3.

4th row K2, [p1, k1] to last 1(0:1:0) st, p1(0:1:0).

These 4 rows form seed st with k2 at front edge.

Work 2(4:6:6) rows more.

Shape neck

Next row (right side) Seed st 27(29:31:33), turn and leave 8(9:10:11) sts on a holder for neck.

Work 1 row.

Dec row (right side) Seed st to last 2 sts, skp.

Cont in seed st, dec in this way at end of next 3(3:4:4) right side rows. 23(25:26:28) sts.

Work 5(5:5:7) rows in seed st.

Bind off.

right front

With size 6 (4mm) needles, cast on 47(50:53:56) sts.

K 5 rows.

Next row (wrong side) P to last 2 sts, k2.

Cont in St st with k2 front edging. Work 10 rows more.

Pocket front

1st row (right side) K11, p1, [k1, p1] 10(11:12:13) times, k15(16:17:18).

2nd row P15(16:17:18), [k1, p1] 10(11:12:13) times, k1, p9, k2.

3rd row K12, [p1, k1] 9(10:11:12) times, p1, k16(17:18:19).

4th row P16(17:18:19), [k1, p1] 9(10:11:12) times, k1, p10, k2.

These 4 rows form seed st for pocket front with St st to each side and k2 front edging.

Work 4 rows more.

Dec row (right side) Patt to last 4 sts, skp, k2.

Cont in patt, dec in this way at end of 2 foll 8th(8th:10th:10th) rows. 44(47:50:53) sts.

Work 2(4:2:4) rows.

Pocket opening row (wrong side) P12(13:14:15), bind off 21(23:25:27) sts of pocket front knitwise, p to last 2 sts, k2.

Place pocket top and lining

Next row (right side) K11, with pocket top in front of pocket lining, k one st of top and one of lining tog each time to make 21(23:25:27) sts, k12(13:14:15). 44(47:50:53) sts.

Cont in St st with k2 front edging, work 3(1:5:3) rows.

Dec at end of next row and on foll 8th(8th:10th:10th) row. 42(45:48:51) sts.
Work 4(6:2:4) rows.

Cord channel

Change to size 3 (3¼mm) needles.

1st row (wrong side) K.

2nd row K3, [yo, k1] to end, yo, taking care not to lose the last yo, turn.

3rd row [K1 tbl, yf, sl1, yb] to last 2 sts, omitting last yb, turn.

4th row [K1, yf, sl1, yb] to end.

5th row [K1, yf, sl1, yb] to last 2 sts, k2.

6th row K3, [yf, sl1, yb, k1] to last st, yf, sl1, yb.

7th row [K1, yf, sl1, yb] to last 2 sts, omitting last yb, turn.

8th row [Skp] to end. 42(45:48:51) sts.

9th row (wrong side) K.

Change to size 6 (4mm) needles.

Beg with a k row, work 2 rows in St st with k2 at front edge.

Inc row (right side) K to last 3 sts, kfb, k2.

Cont in St st with k2 at front edge, inc in this way at end of 4 foll 8th rows. 47(50:53:56) sts.

Work 6(10:14:14) rows.

Shape armhole

Bind off 5 sts at beg of next row.

Dec row (right side) K to last 4 sts, skp, k2.

Cont in St st with k2 at front edge, dec in this way at end of next 6 right side rows. 35(38:41:44) sts.

Work 1(1:1:3) rows.

Yoke

1st row K2, [p1,k1] to last 1(0:1:0) st, p1(0:1:0).

2nd row P0(1:0:1), [k1, p1] to last 3 sts, k3.

3rd row K3, [p1, k1] to last 0(1:0:1) st, p0(1:0:1).

4th row P1(0:1:0), [k1, p1] to last 2 sts, k2.

These 4 rows form seed st with k2 at front edge.

Work 2(4:6:6) rows more.

Shape neck

Next row (right side) Patt 8(9:10:11) and leave these sts on a holder for neck, seed st to end. 27(29:31:33) sts.

Work 1 row.

Dec row (right side) K2tog, seed st to end.

Cont in seed st, dec in this way at beg of next 3(3:4:4) right side rows. 23(25:26:28) sts.

Seed st 5(5:5:7) rows. Bind off.

sleeves

With size 3 (3¼mm) needles, cast on 38(40:44:46) sts.

K 2 rows.

Change to size 6 (4mm) needles.

Beg with a k row, work 6(6:10:12) rows in St st.

Inc row (right side) K1, kfb, k to last 3 sts, kfb, k2.

Cont in St st and inc in this way at each end of 7(7:8:10) foll 8th(10th:10th:8th) rows. 54(56:62:68) sts.

Work 7(7:1:15) rows in St st.

Shape top

Bind off 5 sts at beg of next 2 rows. 44(46:52:58) sts.

Dec row (right side) K2, k2tog, k to last 4 sts, skp, k2.

Dec in this way at each end of next 6 right side rows. 30(32:38:44) sts.

P 1 row.

Bind off.

hood

Back panel

With size 6 (4mm) needles, cast on 19(21:25:27) sts.

Beg with a k row, work 2 rows in St st.

Next row K1, kfb, k to last 3 sts, kfb, k2.

Cont in St st and inc in this way at each end of 3(3:4:4) foll 4th rows. 27(29:35:37) sts.

Work 29(33:37:41) rows in St st.

Dec row (right side) K1, k2tog, k to last 3 sts, skp, k1.

Dec in this way at each end of next 2 right side rows.

P 1 row.

Bind off 2 sts at beg and dec one st at end of next 4 rows. 9(11:17:19) sts.

Bind off.

Front

With size 6 (4mm) circular needle, pick up and k 97(103:115:121) sts around shaped edge of back panel.

Next row (wrong side) K.

Next row K32(34:38:40), kfb, [k2, kfb] 3 times, k12(14:18:20), [kfb, k2] 3 times, kfb, k33(35:39:41). 105(111:123:129) sts.

Beg with a p row, work 17(19:23:25) rows in St st.

Inc row Kfb, k to last 2 sts, kfb, k1.

Cont in St st and inc in this way at each end of 3(3:4:4) foll 4th rows. 113(119:133:139) sts.

P 1 row.

Shape front

1st row (right side) K107(113:127:133), yf, sl1, yb, turn.

2nd row Sl1, p101(107:121:127), sl1, yb, turn.

3rd row Sl1, yb, k96(102:116:122), yf, sl1, yb, turn.

4th row Sl1, p91(97:111:117), sl1, yb, turn.

5th row Sl1, yb, k86(92:106:112), yf, sl1, yb, turn.

6th row Sl1, p81(87:101:107), sl1, yb, turn.

7th row Sl1, yb, k76(82:96:102), yf, sl1, yb, turn.

8th row Sl1, p71(77:91:97), sl1, yb, turn.

9th row Sl1, yb, k66(72:86:92), yf, sl1, yb, turn.

10th row Sl1, p61(67:81:87), sl1, yb, turn.

11th row Sl1, yb, k56(62:76:82), yf, sl1, yb, turn.

12th row Sl1, p51(57:71:77), sl1, yb, turn.

Dec row (right side) Sl1, yb, k3(5:7:9), [k2tog, k2(2:3:3)] 5 times, k2tog, k1(3:3:5), [skp, k2(2:3:3)] 5 times, skp, k4(6:8:10), then k 30 sts from turning rows.

Working on all 101(107:121:127) sts, k 4 rows.

Bind off.

neck edging

Join shoulder seams.

With size 3 (3¼mm) needles, slip 8(9:10:11) sts from right front holder, pick up and k 9(10:11:12) sts up right front neck, 25(27:31:33) sts at center back neck, and 9(10:11:12) sts down left front neck, then patt 6(7:8:9), k2 from holder. 59(65:73:79) sts.

Bind off knitwise.

cord

With size 6 (4mm) needles, cast on 4 sts.

Beg with a k row, work in St st until cord measures 59in/150cm, ending with a k row.

Bind off knitwise.

finishing

Using outline of seed st on Fronts as a guide, slip stitch pocket linings in place. Sew buttons onto pockets and fasten pocket tops. Sew on buttons and fasten back vent. Sew zipper in place. Matching center back of hood to center back of neck and easing to fit, sew hood inside neck edging. Sew sleeves into armholes. Join side and sleeve seams.

Liam

A striking monochrome sweater worked in a double knitting cotton with a Celtic motif. This pattern is not for a beginner, but neither is it as difficult as this may suggest.

measurements	To fit ages	4–6	6–8	8–10	10–12	years
	Actual measurements					
	Length	18	20	22	24	in
		46	51	56	61	cm
	Sleeve	10¾	12¼	13½	14½	in
		27	31	34	37	cm

materials
12(13:15:16) 1¾oz/50g balls of Debbie Bliss cotton dk in Black (A) and two 1¾oz/50g balls Ecru (B)
Pair each size 3 and 6 (U.K. 3¼mm and 4mm) knitting needles

gauge
20 sts and 28 rows to 4in/10cm square over St st using size 6 (4mm) needles.

abbreviations

beg = beginning	**in** = inches	**p** = purl
cm = centimeters	**inc** = increas(e)ing	**skp** = slip 1, knit 1,
cont = continue	**k** = knit	pass slipped stitch over
dec = decreas(e)ing	**kfb** = k into front and	**st(s)** = stitch(es)
foll = following	back of st	**St st** = stockinette stitch

notes

● To work from chart, read 1st and every right side (k) row from right to left, 2nd and every wrong side (p) row from left to right.
● Do not strand yarn—use separate small balls of yarn for each color area and twist yarns when changing colors to avoid holes.
● The outer border of the motif is omitted for 1st and 2nd sizes.

KEY

☐ B

■ A

sweater

front

With size 3 (3¼mm) needles and A, cast on 80(90:100:110) sts.

K 6 rows.

Change to size 6 (4mm) needles.

1st row (right side) K.

2nd row K4, p to last 4 sts, k4.

These 2 rows form St st with k4 at each side for vent edging.

Work 10(10:12:12) more rows to complete vents.

Inc row (right side) Kfb, k to last 2 sts, kfb, k1. 82(92:102:112) sts.

Beg with a p row, work 3(13:15:25) rows in St st. **

Beg at 7th(7th:1st:1st) row and working center 62(62:70:70) sts as indicated, work 88(88:100:100) rows from chart.

With A, work 4(6:6:8) rows in St st.

Shape neck

Next row (right side) K30(35:40:44), turn and work on these sts only for first side.

P 1 row.

Next row K to last 4 sts, skp, k2.

Cont in St st and dec in this way at end of next 4(5:6:7) right side rows. 25(29:33:36) sts.

P 1 row.

Bind off.

With right side facing, slip center 22(22:22:24) sts onto a holder and k to end. 30(35:40:44) sts.

P 1 row.

Next row K2, k2tog, k to end.

Cont in St st and dec in this way at beg of next 4(5:6:7) right side rows. 25(29:33:36) sts.

P 1 row.

Bind off.

back

Work as given for Front to **.
Cont in St st until Back matches Front to shoulder, ending with a p row.
Shape shoulders
Next row (right side) Bind off 25(29:33:36) sts, k until there are 32(34:36:40) sts on right needle, bind off 25(29:33:36).
Leave sts on a holder.

sleeves

With size 3 (3¼mm) needles, cast on 40(42:44:48) sts.
K 6 rows.
Change to size 6 (4mm) needles.
Beg with a k row, work 4 rows in St st.
Inc row (right side) K1, kfb, k to last 3 sts, kfb, k2.
Cont in St st and inc in this way at each end of 9(10:11:11) foll 6th(6th:6th:8th) rows. 60(64:68:72) sts.
P 1 row.
Change to size 3 (3¼mm) needles.
K 6 rows.
Bind off loosely.

neckband

Join left shoulder seam. With right side facing, size 3 (3¼mm) needles, and A, slip 32(34:36:40) sts from back neck holder onto needle, pick up and k 10(11:12:12) sts down left front neck, k 22(22:22:24) sts from center front holder, pick up and k 10(11:12:12) sts up right front neck. 74(78:82:88) sts.
K 6 rows.
Bind off knitwise.

finishing

Join right shoulder and neckband seam. Place markers 6¼(6¾:7:7½)in/ 16(17:18:19)cm down from shoulders on Back and Front. Sew sleeves between markers. Leaving vents open, join side and sleeve seams.

Mia

This is an easy-make jacket in stockinette stitch with picked up ribbing. There are no shoulder or armhole seams, as the body and sleeves are knitted all in one.

measurements							
	To fit ages	3–4	4–5	6–7	8–9	9–10	years
	Actual measurements						
	Chest	31	32	34	36	38	in
		78	82	86	91	96	cm
	Length to shoulder	13¾	14½	15¼	16	17	in
		35	37	39	41	43	cm
	Sleeve length	8¾	9½	10¾	12½	14½	in
		22	24	27	32	37	cm

materials

7(8:8:9:10) 1¾oz/50g balls of Debbie Bliss merino aran
Pair of size 8 (U.K. 5mm) knitting needles
Long size 7 and 8 (U.K. 4½mm and 5mm) circular needles

gauge

18 sts and 24 rows to 4in/10cm square over St st using size 8 (5mm) needles.

abbreviations

alt = alternate   **dec** = decreas(e)ing   **k** = knit
beg = beginning   **foll** = following   **p** = purl
cm = centimeters   **inc** = increas(e)ing   **st(s)** = stitch(es)
cont = continue   **in** = inches   **St st** = stockinette stitch

jacket

Back

With size 8 (5mm) needles, cast on 72(76:80:84:88) sts.

Beg with a k row, work in St st until back measures 7½(8¼:8¾:9:9½)in/19(21:22:23:24)cm from cast-on edge, ending with a p row.

Change to size 8 (5mm) circular needle.

Shape sleeves

Cast on 10(11:12:14:17) sts at beg of next 8 rows. 152(164:176:196:224) sts.

Cont in St st until Back measures 13¾(14½:15¼:16:17)in/35(37:39:41:43)cm from cast-on edge, ending with a p row.

Mark each end of last row with a colored thread to mark shoulder line.

Divide for fronts

Next row (right side) K66(71:76:85:98) sts, bind off next 20(22:24:26:28) sts, k to end.

Cont on last set of sts only for Left Front.

Left Front

Work in St st until same number of rows have been worked as on Back between last set of cast-on sts and shoulder line, ending at sleeve edge.

Shape sleeve

Bind off 10(11:12:14:17) sts at beg of next and 3 foll alt rows. 26(27:28:29:30) sts.

Work even until Front side seam measures same as Back side seam.

Bind off.

Right Front

With wrong side facing, rejoin yarn to rem 66(71:76:88:98) sts, p to end.

Complete to match Left Front, reversing shaping.

edging With right side facing and size 7 (4½mm) circular needle, pick up and k 70(74:78:82:86) sts evenly up Right Front, 26(26:30:30:34) sts at back neck, and 70(74:78:82:86) sts evenly down Left Front. 166(174:186:194:206) sts.
1st row P2, * k2, p2; rep from * to end.
2nd row K2, * p2, k2; rep from * to end.
Rep the last 2 rows for 4(4:4¼:4¼:4¾)in/10(10:11:11:12)cm, ending with a 2nd row.
Bind off loosely in rib.

finishing Join side and sleeve seams.

Pea

This is a double-breasted nautical-style coat with revers, which is knitted in a soft merino aran.

	To fit	3–4	5–6	7–8	9–10	years
measurements	**Actual measurements**					
	Chest	26	28¼	30	32¾	in
		66	72	76	83	cm
	Length to shoulder	16½	19	21¾	23½	in
		42	48	55	60	cm
	Sleeve length	10¼	11½	13	15¾	in
		26	29	33	40	cm

materials

10(12:13:14) 1¾oz/50g balls of Debbie Bliss merino aran in Ultramarine
Pair each size 7 and 8 (U.K. 4½mm and 5mm) knitting needles
6 buttons

gauge

18 sts and 24 rows to 4in/10cm square over St st using size 8 (5mm) needles.
22 sts and 26 rows to 4in/10cm square over patt using size 7 (4½mm) needles.

abbreviations

beg = beginning	**in** = inches	**rem** = remain(ing)
cm = centimeters	**inc** = increas(e)ing	**rep** = repeat
cont = continue	**k** = knit	**st(s)** = stitch(es)
dec = decreas(e)ing	**p** = purl	**yo** = yarn over
foll = following	**patt** = pattern	

coat

back

With size 8 (5mm) needles, cast on 74(82:86:94) sts.
1st row P2, * k2, p2; rep from * to end.
2nd row K2, * p2, k2; rep from * to end.
These 2 rows form the rib patt.
Cont in patt until Back measures 5½(6¼:7½:8¼)in/14(16:19:21)cm from cast-on

edge, ending with a wrong side row.

Change to size 7 (4½mm) needles.

Cont in rib patt until Back measures 10¾(12½:15:16)in/27(32:38:41)cm from cast-on edge, ending with a wrong side row.

Shape armholes

Bind off 4(6:6:8) sts at beg of next 2 rows. 66(70:74:78) sts.

Dec one st at each end of the next 3 rows. 60(64:68:72) sts.

Cont in patt until Back measures 16½(19:21¾:23½)in/42(48:55:60)cm from cast-on edge, ending with a wrong side row.

Shape shoulders

Bind off 9(10:10:11) sts at beg of next 2 rows and 9(9:10:10) sts at beg of next 2 rows.

Bind off rem 24(26:28:30) sts.

left front

With size 8 (5mm) needles, cast on 49(53:57:61) sts.

1st row P2, * k2, p2; rep from * to last 3 sts, k3.

2nd row K1, * p2, k2; rep from * to end.

These 2 rows form the rib patt.

Cont in patt until Front measures 5½(6¼:7½:8¼)in/14(16:19:21)cm from cast-on edge, ending with a wrong side row.

Change to size 7 (4½mm) needles.

Cont in rib patt until Front measures 10¾(12½:15:16)in/27(32:38:41)cm from cast-on edge, ending with a wrong side row.

Shape armholes

Bind off 4(6:6:8) sts at beg of next row. 45(47:51:53) sts.

Work 1 row.

Dec one st at armhole edge of the next 3 rows. 42(44:48:50) sts.

Work even in patt until Front measures 14½(17:19¾:21¾)in/37(43:50:55)cm from cast-on edge, ending at neck edge.

Shape neck

Next row Bind off 20(21:24:25) sts, patt to end.

Dec one st at neck edge of next 4 rows. 18(19:20:21) sts.

Work even until Front measures same as Back to shoulder, ending at armhole edge.

Shape shoulder

Bind off 9(10:10:11) sts at beg of next row.

Work 1 row.

Bind off rem 9(9:10:10) sts.

Place markers for three pairs of buttons—the first pair 5½(6¼:7½:8¼)in/14(16: 19:21)cm from cast-on edge, the third pair 4¼(4¾:5:5½)in/11(12:13:14)cm below neck edge, and the remaining pair spaced halfway between.

right front

With size 8 (5mm) needles, cast on 49(53:57:61) sts.

1st row K3, p2, * k2, p2; rep from * to end.

2nd row K2, * p2, k2; rep from * to last 3 sts, p2, k1.

These 2 rows form the rib patt.

Working buttonholes on right side rows to match markers, complete to match Left Front.

Buttonhole row Rib 5, yo, k2tog, rib 20, yo, p2tog, rib to end.

sleeves

With size 7 (4½mm) needles, cast on 42(46:46:50) sts.

1st row K2, * p2, k2; rep from * to end.

2nd row P2, * k2, p2; rep from * to end.

These 2 rows form the rib patt.

Work a further 8 rows.

Change to size 8 (5mm) needles.

Cont in patt *at the same time* inc and work into patt one st at each end of the next and every foll 4th row until there are 64(74:78:88) sts.

Work even until sleeve measures 10¼(11½:13:15¾)in/26(29:33:40)cm from cast-on edge, ending with a wrong side row.

Shape sleeve top

Bind off 4(6:6:8) sts at beg of next 2 rows. 56(62:66:72) sts.

Dec one st at each end of the next 3 rows. 50(56:60:66) sts.

Bind off 4 sts at beg of next 2(2:0:0) rows.

Bind off 3 sts at beg of next 10(12:16:18) rows.

Bind off rem 12 sts in patt.

collar

Join shoulder seams.

With wrong side of Left Front facing and size 7 (4½mm) needles, skip first 10 bound-off sts, pick up and k 10(11:14:15) sts from rem bound-off sts, pick up and k 10 sts up Left Front neck to shoulder, 24(26:28:30) sts from back neck, 10 sts down Right Front neck, and first 10(11:14:15) sts bound off at Right Front. 64(68:76:80) sts.

1st row K1, p2, * k2, p2; rep from * to last st, k1.

2nd row K3, * p2, k2, rep from * to last 5 sts, p2, k3.

3rd and 4th sizes only

Next 2 rows Rib to last 24 sts, turn.

All sizes

Next 2 rows Rib to last 20 sts, turn.

Next 2 rows Rib to last 16 sts, turn.

Next 2 rows Rib to last 12 sts, turn.

Work a further 2in/5cm in rib across all sts.

Bind off in rib.

finishing

Sew sleeves into armholes. Join side and sleeve seams. Sew on buttons to match buttonholes.

sid

A butcher's boy hat incoporating cables and a crocheted brim. The hat is knitted in a denim aran yarn to give it a stylishly retro look.

size
To fit 20–22in/51–56cm around head

materials
Four 1¾oz/50g balls of Debbie Bliss cotton denim aran in Medium Blue
Pair of size 6 (4mm) knitting needles
Size E–4 (U.K. 3.50mm) crochet hook
Cable needle

gauge
19 sts and 28 rows to 4in/10cm over rev St st using size 6 (4mm) needles.

abbreviations

C2F = slip next st onto cable needle and hold at front, k1, k1 from cable needle
C4B = slip next 2 sts onto cable needle and hold at back, k2, k2 from cable needle
C4F = slip next 2 sts onto cable needle and hold at front, k2, k2 from cable needle

ch = chain
cm = centimeters
cont = continue
dec = decreas(e)ing
in = inches
k = knit
M1 = make one by picking up the loop lying between st just worked and next st and working into the back of it

p = purl
patt = pattern
rev St st = reverse stockinette stitch
sc = single crochet (called double crochet or dc in U.K.)
skp = slip 1, knit 1, pass slipped stitch over
ss = slip stitch
st(s) = stitch(es)
tog = together

hat

note

● If necessary, change crochet hook size to give a neat edge that lies flat for the band and use the same size for the brim.

to make

With size 6 (4mm) needles, cast on 122 sts.

1st row (right side) P1, [C4B, k2, p14] 6 times, p1.

2nd and 4th rows K1, [k14, p6] 6 times, k1.

3rd row P1, [k2, C4F, p14] 6 times, p1.

These 4 rows form panels of plait cables and rev St st. Work 1 row.

6th row (wrong side) K1, [M1, k4, M1, k6, M1, k4, M1, p6] 6 times, k1. 146 sts.

7th row P1, [k2, C4F, p18] 6 times, p1.

8th row K1, [M1, k18, M1, p6] 6 times, k1. 158 sts.

9th row P1, [C4B, k2, p20] 6 times, p1.

10th row K1, [M1, k20, M1, p6] 6 times, k1. 170 sts.

Work 25 rows in patt as set.

Shape top

Keeping plait cables correct, work as follows:

1st row (wrong side) K1, [skp, k18, k2tog, p6] 6 times, k1. 158 sts.

Work 3 rows in patt.

5th row K1, [skp, k16, k2tog, p6] 6 times, k1. 146 sts.

Work 3 rows in patt.

9th row K1, [skp, k14, k2tog, p6] 6 times, k1. 134 sts.

Work 1 row in patt.

11th row K1, [skp, k12, k2tog, p6] 6 times, k1. 122 sts.

Cont in patt, working 2 sts less between skp and k2tog, dec 2 sts in each panel on next 5 wrong side rows. 62 sts.

Work 1 row in patt.

23rd row K1, [skp, k2tog, p6] 6 times, k1. 50 sts.

24th row P1, [k2, slip next 2 sts onto cable needle, hold at front, k2, k2tog from cable needle, p2] 6 times, p1. 44 sts.

25th row K1, [k2tog, p5] 6 times, k1. 38 sts.

26th row P1, [slip next 2 sts onto cable needle, hold at back, skp, k2 from cable needle, k1, p1] 6 times, p1. 32 sts.

27th row K2, [p1, p2tog, p1, k1] 6 times. 26 sts.

28th row P1, k1, [C2F, k2tog] 5 times, C2F, p2tog. 20 sts.

29th row K1, [p1, p2tog] 6 times, k1. 14 sts.

30th row P1, [skp] 6 times, p1. 8 sts.
Leaving a long end, cut yarn. Thread end through sts, draw up, and secure.

band

With wrong side facing and size E–4 (3.50mm) crochet hook, join yarn in first st.
1st row (wrong side) Ch1, 1sc in first st, [3sc over 6 sts of cable, skip one st, 1sc in each of next 12 sts, skip one st] 6 times, 1sc in last st. 92sc.
2nd row Ch1, 1sc in each sc to end.
Work 3 rows more in sc. Fasten off.

brim

With size E–4 (3.5mm) hook and with wrong side facing, join yarn in 43rd sc.
1st row Ch1, 1sc in each of next 3sc, slip st in each of next 2sc, turn.
2nd row 2sc in each of 3sc of peak, slip st in ch, slip st in next sc of band, turn.
3rd row 2sc in each sc of peak, slip st in each of next 2sc of band, turn.
4th, 5th, 6th, 7th, 8th, 9th, and 10th rows 2sc in first sc of peak, 1sc in each sc to last sc of peak, 2sc in last sc, slip st in each of next 2sc of band, turn.
11th row 2sc in first sc of peak, 1sc in each of next 5sc, 2sc in each of next 2sc, 1sc in each sc to last 8sc of peak, 2sc in each of next 2sc, 1sc in each of next 5sc, 2sc in last sc of peak, slip st in each of next 2sc of band, turn.
12th, 13th, 14th, 15th, and 16th rows As 4th row.
Fasten off.

finishing

Join back seam. Press according to yarn label, using a small amount of spray starch to stiffen brim. Make a 2in/5cm pompon and sew on top.

pompon

1 Cut two circles from cardboard that are slightly smaller than the diameter of the pompon required. Make a central hole through both circles approximately one-third of the diameter. Place both rings together, one on top of the other, lining up the holes.
2 Thread yarn though a darning needle and wind the yarn through the hole and around the outer edge, ensuring that all the cardboard is covered. Continue until the hole in the center is completely filled and it is impossible to force the needle through the center. This will ensure that the pompon is as firm and neat as possible.
3 Ease the two circles apart and cut all the strands between the circles. Do not remove the cardboard until a tightly tied double strand of yarn has been secured around the center of all the strands, leaving a length free to sew the pompon in place. Remove the cardboard and trim any straggly ends of yarn.

Max

This baseball-style jacket with a zipper has a star motif for the new sheriff in town. It is knitted in a soft merino aran for warmth and practicality.

measurements								
	To fit	4–5	5–6	6–7	7–8	8–9	9–10	years
	Actual measurements							
	Chest	31½	33	34½	36½	38½	40¼	in
		80	84	88	93	98	102	cm
	Length to shoulder	16½	17¼	19	19¾	21¾	23¾	in
		42	44	48	50	55	60	cm
	Sleeve length	10¼	11	11¾	12½	13¾	15¾	in
		26	28	30	32	35	40	cm

materials

5(6:6:7:7:8) 1¾oz/50g balls of Debbie Bliss merino aran in main color Grey (MC) and 3(3:4:4:5:5) balls in contrasting color Red (CC)
Pair each size 7 and 8 (U.K. 4½mm and 5mm) knitting needles
14(14:16:16:18:18)in/35(35:40:40:45:45)cm open-ended zipper

gauge

18 sts and 24 rows to 4in/10cm square over St st using size 8 (5mm) needles.

abbreviations

beg = beginning   **in** = inches   **rem** = remain(ing)
cm = centimeters   **k** = knit   **rep** = repeat
cont = continue   **p** = purl   **st(s)** = stitch(es)
dec = decreas(e)ing   **patt** = pattern   **St st** = stockinette stitch

jacket

back

With size 7 (4½mm) needles and CC, cast on 74(78:82:86:90:94) sts.

1st, 3rd, and 5th sizes only

1st rib row K2, * p2, k2; rep from * to end.

2nd rib row P2, * k2, p2; rep from * to end.

2nd, 4th, and 6th sizes only

1st rib row P2, * k2, p2; rep from * to end.

2nd rib row K2, * p2, k2; rep from * to end.

All sizes

These 2 rows form the rib.

Cont in rib and work 2 rows MC, 2 rows CC, and 2 rows MC.

Change to size 8 (5mm) needles.

Beg with a k row, work in St st and MC only until back measures 10¾(11:12¼:12½:14¼:15¾)in/27(28:31:32:36:40)cm from cast-on edge, ending with a wrong side row.

Shape armhole

Bind off 5(5:6:6:7:7) sts at beg of next 2 rows. 64(68:70:74:76:80) sts.

Work even until Back measures 15¼(16:17¾:18½:20½:22½)in/ 39(41:45:47:52:57)cm from cast-on edge, ending with a p row.

Shape back neck

Next row K23(24:25:26:27:28) sts, turn and work on these sts for first side of back neck.

Dec one st at neck edge of the next 4 rows.

Work even for 3 rows.

Shape shoulder

Bind off 10(10:11:11:12:12) sts at beg of next row.

Work 1 row.

Bind off rem 9(10:10:11:11:12) sts.

With right side facing, slip center 18(20:20:22:22:24) sts onto a holder, rejoin yarn to rem sts, k to end.

Dec one st at neck edge of the next 4 rows.

Work even for 4 rows.

Shape shoulder

Bind off 10(10:11:11:12:12) sts at beg of next row.

Work 1 row.

Bind off rem 9(10:10:11:11:12) sts.

left front

With size 7 (4½mm) needles and CC, cast on 35(37:39:41:43:45) sts.

1st, 3rd, and 5th sizes only

1st rib row (right side) K2, * p2, k2; rep from * to last 5 sts, p2, k3.

2nd rib row P3, * k2, p2; rep from * to end.

2nd, 4th, and 6th sizes only

1st rib row (right side) P2, * k2, p2, rep from * to last 3 sts, k3.

2nd rib row P3, * k2, p2; rep from * to last 2 sts.

All sizes

These 2 rows form the rib.

Cont in rib and work 2 rows MC, 2 rows CC, and 2 rows MC.

Change to size 8 (5mm) needles.

Beg with a k row, work in St st and MC only until Front measures 10¾(11:12¼:12½:14¼:15¾)in/27(28:31:32:36:40)cm from cast-on edge, ending with a p row.

Shape armhole

Bind off 5(5:6:6:7:7) sts at beg of next row. 30(32:33:35:36:38) sts.

Work even until Front measures 15(15¼:17:17¼:19:21)in/38(39:43:44:48:53)cm from cast-on edge, ending with a k row.

Shape neck

Next row P8, slip these 8 sts onto a holder, p to end.

Dec one st at neck edge on every row until 19(20:21:22:23:24) sts rem.

Work even until Front measures same as Back to shoulder, ending at side edge.

Shape shoulder

Bind off 10(10:11:11:12:12) sts at beg of next row.

Work 1 row.

Bind off rem 9(10:10:11:11:12) sts.

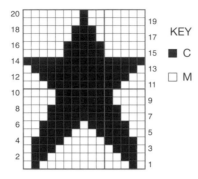

KEY

■ C

□ M

right front

With size 7 (4½mm) needles and CC, cast on 35(37:39:41:43:45) sts.

1st, 3rd, and 5th sizes only

1st rib row (right side) K3, * p2, k2; rep from * to end.

2nd rib row P2, * k2, p2; rep from * to last 5 sts, k2, p3.

2nd, 4th, and 6th sizes only

1st rib row (right side) K3, * p2, k2, rep from * to last 2 sts, p2.

2nd rib row K2, * p2, k2; rep from * to last 3 sts, p3.

All sizes

These 2 rows form the rib.

Cont in rib and work 2 rows MC, 2 rows CC, and 2 rows MC.

Change to size 8 (5mm) needles.

Beg with a k row, work in St st and MC only until Front measures 10¾(11:12¼:12½:14¼:15¾)in/27(28:31:32:36:40)cm from cast-on edge, ending with a k row.

Shape armhole

Bind off 5(5:6:6:7:7) sts at beg of next row. 30(32:33:35:36:38) sts.

Next row K7(8:9:10:10:11)MC, k across 15 sts of 1st row of Chart, k8(9:9:10:11:12)MC.

This row sets the position of the chart, cont in St st until all 20 rows of chart have been worked.

Work even until Front measures 15(15¼:17:17¼:19:21)in/38(39: 43:44:48:53)cm from cast-on edge, ending with a p row.

Shape neck

Next row K8, slip these 8 sts onto a holder, k to end.

Dec one st at neck edge on every row until 19(20:21:22:23:24) sts rem.

Work even until Front measures same as Back to shoulder, ending at side edge.

Shape shoulder

Bind off 10(10:11:11:12:12) sts at beg of next row.

Work 1 row.

Bind off rem 9(10:10:11:11:12) sts.

sleeves

With size 7 (4½mm) needles and CC, cast on 30(34:38:38:42:42) sts.

1st rib row K2, * p2, k2; rep from * to end.

2nd rib row P2, * k2, p2; rep from * to end.

These 2 rows form the rib.

Cont in rib and work 2 rows MC, 2 rows CC and 6 rows MC.

Change to size 8 (5mm) needles.

Beg with a k row, work in St st and CC only.

Inc one st at each end of the 3rd and every foll 4th row until there are 54(60:64:68:74:78) sts.

Work even until sleeve measures 10¼(11:11¾:12½:13¾:15¾)in/26(28:30:32:35:40)cm from cast-on edge, ending with a p row.

Mark each end of last row with a colored thread.

Work a further 6(6:8:8:10:10) rows.

Bind off.

collar

Join shoulder seams.

With right side facing, size 7 (4½mm) needles, and MC, slip 8 sts from right front holder onto needle, pick up and k 12(13:13:14:16:17) sts up right front neck, 11 sts down right back neck, k 18(20:20:22:22:24) sts from back neck holder, pick up and k 11 sts up left back neck, 12(13:13:14:16:17) sts down left front neck, then k8 from left front holder. 80(84:84:88:92:96) sts.

Next row P3, * k2, p2; rep from * to last 5 sts, k2, p3.

Next row K3, * p2, k2; rep from * to last 5 sts, p2, k3.

Work a further 1½(1½:2:2:2:2)in/4(4:5:5:5:5)cm in rib patt as set, ending with a right side row.

Work 2 rows CC, 2 rows MC, 2 rows CC.

Bind off in rib.

front edgings

With right side facing, size 7 (4½mm) needles, and CC, pick up and k 84(86:97:99:105:114) sts along left front edge.

K 1 row.

Bind off.

Repeat for right front edge.

finishing

With center of bound-off edge of sleeve to shoulder seam, sew sleeves into armholes, with row ends above markers sewn to bound-off sts at underarm. Join side and sleeve seams. Sew in zipper.

Molly

A delicious pastel bolero worked all in one so there are no armhole seams. It is knitted in a cashmere mix so that it is light and beautifully soft.

measurements							
To fit ages		3–4	4–5	6–7	8–9	9–10	years
Actual measurements							
Chest		31	32	34	36	38	in
		78	82	86	91	96	cm
Length to shoulder		11	11¾	12¼	13	13¾	in
		28	30	31	33	35	cm
Sleeve length		8¾	9¾	11	11¾	14¼	in
(with cuff turned back)		22	25	28	30	36	cm

materials

5(6:7:7:8) 1¾oz/50g balls of Debbie Bliss cashmerino aran in Pale Pink
Pair each size 7 and 8 (U.K. 4½mm and 5mm) knitting needles
Long size 7 and 8 (U.K. 4½mm and 5mm) circular needles

gauge

18 sts and 24 rows to 4in/10cm square over St st using size 8 (5mm) needles.

abbreviations

alt = alternate
beg = beginning
cm = centimeters
cont = continue
foll = following
in = inches
inc = increas(e)ing

k = knit
M1 = make one by picking up the loop lying between st just worked and next st and working into the back of it

p = purl
rem = remain(ing)
rep = repeat
skp = slip 1, knit 1, pass slipped stitch over
st(s) = stitch(es)
St st = stockinette stitch
tog = together

bolero

back, fronts and sleeves

(worked in one piece)

With size 8 (5mm) needles, cast on 72(76:80:84:88) sts.

Beg with a k row, work 22(24:26:28:30) rows in St st.

Change to size 8 (5mm) circular needle.

Shape sleeves

Cast on 8(9:10:11:13) sts at beg of next 8 rows. 136(148:160:172:192) sts.

Work 30(32:34:36:38) rows in St st.

Mark each end of last row with a colored thread to mark shoulder line.

Divide for fronts

Next row (right side) K 58(63:68:73:82) sts, bind off next 20(22:24:26:28) sts, k to end.

Cont on last set of sts for left front, leave rem sts on a spare needle.

Left Front

Work even for 5(5:7:7:9) rows, so ending at front edge.

Next row K3, M1, k to end.

Work even for 3 rows.

Rep the last 4 rows 4(5:5:6:6) times more and then the inc row once more. 64(70:75:81:90) sts.

Work 4(2:2:0:0) rows in St st, ending at sleeve edge.

Sleeve shaping

Bind off 8(9:10:11:13) sts at beg of next and 3 foll alt rows. 32(34:35:37:38) sts.

Work even for 4 rows.

Shape front

Next row (right side) K1, skp, k to end.

Next row P to end.

Rep the last 2 rows 3(4:5:6:7) times more.

Next row Bind off 2 sts, k to end.

Next row P to end.

Next row Bind off 3 sts, k to end.

Next row P to end.

Next row Bind off 4 sts, k to end.

Next row P to end.

Next row Bind off 5 sts, k to end.

Next row P to end.

Next row Bind off 6 sts, k to end.

Next row P to end.

Leave rem 8(9:9:10:10) sts on a holder.

Right Front

With wrong side facing, rejoin yarn to rem sts on spare needle, p to end.

Work even for 4(4:6:6:8) rows, ending at sleeve edge.

Next row K to last 3 sts, M1, k3.

Work even for 3 rows.

Rep the last 4 rows 4(5:5:6:6) times more and then the inc row once more. 64(70:75:81:90) sts.

Work 5(3:3:1:1) rows in St st, ending at sleeve edge.

Sleeve shaping

Bind off 8(9:10:11:13) sts at beg of next and 3 foll alt rows. 32(34:35:37:38) sts.

Work even for 3 rows.

Shape front

Next row (right side) K to last 3 sts, k2tog, k1.

Next row P to end.

Rep the last 2 rows 3(4:5:6:7) times more.

Next row K to end.

Next row Bind off 2 sts, p to end.

Next row K to end.

Next row Bind off 3 sts, p to end.

Next row K to end.

Next row Bind off 4 sts, p to end.

Next row K to end.

Next row Bind off 5 sts, p to end.

Next row K to end.

Next row Bind off 6 sts, p to end.

Leave rem 8(9:9:10:10) sts on a holder.

front edging and collar

With right side facing and size 7 (4½mm) circular needle, beginning at lower right front edge, k 8(9:9:10:10) sts from holder, pick up and k 33(35:37:39:41) sts evenly around right front edge to top of lower front shaping,16 sts along straight edge, 26(28:30:32:34) sts up right front neck to shoulder, 24(26:30:32:36) sts from back neck, 26(28:30:32:34) sts down left front neck, 16 sts along straight edge, and k 33(35:37:39:41) sts evenly around shaped lower front edge, then k 8(9:9:10:10) sts from holder. 190(202:214:226:238) sts.

1st row (wrong side) P2, * k2, p2; rep from * to end.

Working in rib as set, cont as follows:

Next 2 rows Rib to last 81(86:90:95:99) sts, turn.

Next 2 rows Rib to last 77(82:85:89:94) sts, turn.

Next 2 rows Rib to last 73(78:80:84:89) sts, turn.

Next 2 rows Rib to last 69(74:75:79:84) sts, turn.

Next 2 rows Rib to last 65(69:71:74:79) sts, turn.

40

Next 2 rows Rib to last 61(64:66:69:74) sts, turn.
Next row Rib to end.
Work a further 7 rows in rib.
Bind off in rib.

lower back edging

With right side facing and size 7 (4½mm) needles, pick up and k 70(74:78:82:86) sts along lower back edge.
1st row (wrong side) P2, * k2, p2; rep from * to end.
2nd row K2, * p2, k2; rep from * to end.
Rep the last 2 rows 3 times more and the 1st row again.
Bind off in rib.

cuffs

With right side facing and size 7 (4½mm) needles, pick up and k 46(50:54:58:62) sts along sleeve edge.
1st row (wrong side) P2, * k2, p2; rep from * to end.
2nd row K2, * p2, k2; rep from * to end.
Rep the last 2 rows for 2(2:2¼:2¼:2¾)in/5(5:6:6:7)cm.
Change to size 8 (5mm) needles.
Work a further 2(2:2¼:2¼:2¾)in/5(5:6:6:7)cm in rib.
Bind off in rib.

finishing

Join side and sleeve seams, reversing seam on cuff.

Beth

A cabled jacket with deep rib fronts fastened with leather ties. It is knitted in a classic tweed yarn with bright flecks.

measurements	To fit	3–5	6–8	9–10	years
	Actual measurements				
	Chest	31½	35	37¾	in
		80	88	96	cm
	Length to shoulder	15	16½	18½	in
		38	42	47	cm
	Sleeve length	9½	11	13¾	in
		24	28	35	cm

materials

9(10:11) 1¾oz/50g balls of Debbie Bliss aran tweed in Grey
Pair each size 7 and 8 (U.K. 4½mm and 5mm) knitting needles
Long size 7 (U.K. 4½mm) circular needle
Cable needle
19¾in/50cm of narrow leather strip

gauges

18 sts and 24 rows to 4in/10cm square over St st using size 8 (5mm) needles.
23 sts and 26 rows 4in/10cm square over patt using size 8 (5mm) needles.

abbreviations

beg = beginning
C4F = slip next 2 sts onto cable needle and leave at front of work, k2, then k2 from cable needle

cm = centimeters
cont = continue
dec = decreas(e)ing
foll = following
in = inches
inc = increas(e)ing

k = knit
p = purl
patt = pattern
rem = remain(ing)
rep = repeat
st(s) = stitch(es)

jacket

back

With size 7 (4½mm) needles, cast on 92(102:112) sts.

1st row K2, * p2, k4, p2, k2; rep from * to end.

2nd row P2, * k2, p4, k2, p2; rep from * to end.

3rd row K2, * p2, C4F, p2, k2; rep from * to end.

4th row P2, * k2, p4, k2, p2; rep from * to end.

These 4 rows form the cable and rib patt.

Change to size 8 (5mm) needles.

Cont in patt until Back measures 9¾(10¾:11¾)in/25(27:30)cm from cast-on edge, ending with a wrong side row.

Shape armholes

Bind off 3 sts at beg of next 2 rows. 86(96:106) sts.

Cont in patt until Back measures 15(16½:18½)in/38(42:47)cm from cast-on edge, ending with a wrong side row.

Shape shoulders

Bind off 15(17:18) sts at beg of next 2 rows and 15(16:18) sts at beg of foll 2 rows.

Bind off rem 26(30:34) sts.

left front

With size 7 (4½mm) needles, cast on 41(41:41) sts.

1st row K2, * p2, k4, p2, k2; rep from * to last 9 sts, p2, k7.

2nd row K3, p4, k2, p2, * k2, p4, k2, p2; rep from * to end.

3rd row K2, * p2, C4F, p2, k2; rep from * to last 9 sts, p2, C4F, k3.

4th row K3, p4, k2, p2 * k2, p4, k2, p2; rep from * to end.

These 4 rows form the cable and rib patt.

Change to size 8 (5mm) needles.

Cont in patt until Front measures 9¾(10¾:11¾)in/25(27:30)cm from cast-on edge, ending with a wrong side row.

Shape armhole

Bind off 3 sts at beg of next row. 38(38:38) sts.

Patt 1 row.

Shape neck

Dec one st at neck edge on next and every foll 4th(6th:16th) row until 30(33:36) sts rem.

Work even until Front measures same as Back to shoulder, ending with a wrong side row.

Shape shoulder

Bind off 15(17:18) sts at beg of next row.

Work 1 row.

Bind off rem 15(16:18) sts.

right front

With size 7 (4½mm) needles, cast on 41(41:41)sts.

1st row K7, p2, k2, * p2, k4, p2, k2; rep from * end.

2nd row P2, * k2, p4, k2, p2; rep from * to last 9 sts, k2, p4, k3.

3rd row K3, C4F, p2, k2, * p2, C4F, p2, k2; rep from * to end.

4th row P2, * k2, p4, k2, p2; rep from * to last 9 sts, k2, p4, k3.

These 4 rows form the cable and rib patt.

Change to size 8 (5mm) needles.

Cont in patt until Front measures 9¾(10¾:11¾)in/25(27:30)cm from cast-on edge, ending with a right side row.

Shape armhole

Bind off 3 sts at beg of next row. 38(38:38) sts.

Shape neck

Dec one st at neck edge on next and every foll 4th(6th:16th) row until 30(33:36) sts rem.

Work even until Front measures same as Back to shoulder, ending with a right side row.

Shape shoulder

Bind off 15(17:18) sts at beg of next row.

Work 1 row.

Bind off rem 15(16:18) sts.

sleeves

With size 7 (4½mm) needles, cast on 42(52:62) sts.

1st row K2, * p2, k4, p2, k2; rep from * to end.

2nd row P2, * k2, p4, k2, p2; rep from * to end.

3rd row K2, * p2, C4F, p2, k2; rep from * to end.

4th row P2, * k2, p4, k2, p2; rep from * to end.

These 4 rows form the cable and rib patt.

Work a further 8 rows.

Change to size 8 (5mm) needles.

Cont in patt *at the same time* inc and work into patt, one st at each end of the 3rd and every foll 5th(6th:5th) row until there are 60(70:84) sts.

Work even until sleeve measures 9½(11:13¾)in/24(28:35)cm from cast-on edge, ending with a wrong side row.

Mark each end of last row with a colored thread.

Work a further 4 rows.

Bind off in patt.

front bands and collar

Join shoulder seams.

With right side facing and size 7 (4½mm) circular needle, pick up and k 48(54:60) sts evenly up Right Front to beg of neck shaping, 26(30:36) sts to shoulder, 26(30:34) sts across back neck, 26(30:36) sts down Left Front to beg of neck shaping, and 48(54:60) sts to cast-on edge. 174(198:226) sts.

1st row (wrong side) P2, * k2, p2; rep from * to end.

Cont to work turning rows as follows in k2, p2 rib as set:

3rd size only

Next 2 rows Rib to last 92 sts, turn.

Next 2 rows Rib to last 88 sts, turn.

Next 2 rows Rib to last 84 sts, turn.

2nd and 3rd sizes only

Next 2 rows Rib to last 80 sts, turn.

Next 2 rows Rib to last 76 sts, turn.

Next 2 rows Rib to last 72 sts, turn.

All sizes

Next 2 rows Rib to last 68 sts, turn.

Next 2 rows Rib to last 64 sts, turn.

Next 2 rows Rib to last 60 sts, turn.

Next 2 rows Rib to last 56 sts, turn.

Next row Rib to end.

Work in rib for a further 4(4¾:6)in/10(12:15)cm, ending with a wrong side row. Bind off loosely but evenly in rib.

finishing

Sew sleeves into armholes with row ends above markers sewn to cast-off sts of underarm. Join side and sleeve seams. Cut leather strip in half, overlap the front pieces of the jacket, and stitch leather strips in place.

Sam

A fisherman's vest with pockets and a zipper is stylish and practical. The gilet is knitted in cotton, which enhances the subtle diamond stitch.

measurements	To fit ages	3–4	5–6	7–8	years
	Actual measurements				
	Chest	32	33½	35½	in
		81	85	90	cm
	Length	14½	15¾	17	in
		37	40	43	cm

materials

7(8:9) 1¾oz/50g balls of Debbie Bliss cotton dk in Chocolate
Pair each size 3 and 6 (U.K. 3¼mm and 4mm) knitting needles
18(18:20)in/46(46:51)cm open-ended zipper
4 buttons

gauge

18 sts and 28 rows to 4in/10cm square over patt using size 6 (4mm) needles.

abbreviations

beg = beginning
cm = centimeters
cont = continue
dec = decreas(e)ing
in = inches

k = knit
p = purl
patt = pattern
skp = slip 1, knit 1,
pass slipped stitch over

st(s) = stitch(es)
St st = stockinette stitch
tog = together
yo = yarn over

waistcoat

note

● To work in patt from chart, read 1st and every right side row from right to left, 2nd and every wrong side row from left to right.

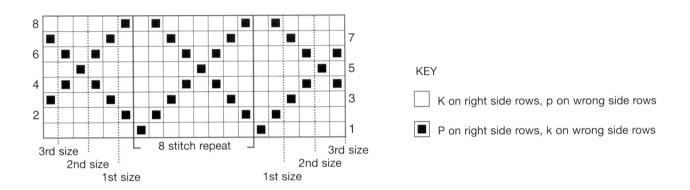

KEY

☐ K on right side rows, p on wrong side rows

■ P on right side rows, k on wrong side rows

back

With size 3 (3¼mm) needles, cast on 75(79:83) sts.

1st row (right side) K1, [p1, k1] to end.

This row forms seed st.

Work 3 rows more in seed st.

Change to size 6 (4mm) needles.

Beg and ending as indicated, work in patt from chart for 60(64:68) rows, so ending with 4th(8th:4th) row of 8th(8th:9th) patt repeat.

Shape armholes

Keeping patt correct throughout, bind off 5 sts at beg of next 2 rows.

Dec row (right side) K2tog, patt to last 2 sts, skp.

Dec in this way on next 2(3:4) right side rows. 59(61:63) sts.

Patt 34(36:38) rows, so ending with a right side row.

Bind off.

large pocket linings

(make 2)

With size 6 (4mm) needles, cast on 17 sts.

Beg with a k row, work 15(17:19) rows in St st, so ending with a k row.

Leave sts on a holder.

small pocket linings

(make 2)

With size 6 (4mm) needles, cast on 15 sts.

Beg with a k row, work 7(9:11) rows in St st, so ending with a k row.

Leave sts on a holder.

left front

With size 3 (3¼mm) needles, cast on 37(39:41) sts.

Work 4 rows in seed st as for Back.

Change to size 6 (4mm) needles.

Work in patt from chart as follows:

1st row (right side) Beg as indicated for size, work 2(4:6) edge sts, [repeat 8 sts] 4 times, seed st 3.

This row sets patt from chart.

Omitting edge sts on the left of the chart and working 3 sts in seed st at front edge on every row, work 20(22:24) rows in patt.

1st pocket opening row (wrong side) Patt 11, slip next 17 sts onto a holder, patt 17 sts of large pocket lining, patt 9(11:13). 37(39:41) sts.

Patt 38(40:42) rows more, so ending with 4th(8th:4th) row of 8th(8th:9th) patt.

Shape armhole

Bind off 5 sts at beg of next row.

Patt 1 row.

Dec row (right side) K2tog, patt to end.

Cont in patt, dec in this way at beg of next 2(3:4) right side rows. 29(30:31) sts.

Patt 14(10:6) rows.

2nd pocket opening row (wrong side) Patt 8, slip next 15 sts onto a holder, patt 15 sts of small pocket lining, patt 6(7:8). 29(30:31) sts.

Patt 10(12:14) rows.

Shape neck

Next row (right side) Patt 23(24:25), turn and leave 6 sts on a holder for collar.

Dec one st at neck edge on next 8 rows. 15(16:17) sts.

Patt 0(4:8) rows, so ending with a right side row.

Bind off.

right front

With size 3 (3¼mm) needles, cast on 37(39:41) sts.

Work 4 rows in seed st as for Back.

Change to size 6 (4mm) needles.

1st row (right side) Seed st 3, omitting edge sts on right of chart, [repeat 8 sts] 4 times, work 2(4:6) edge sts.

2nd row Work 2(4:6) edge sts at left of chart, [repeat 8 sts] 4 times, seed st 3.

These 2 rows set patt from chart.

Omitting edge sts on the right of chart and working 3 sts in seed st at front edge on every row, patt 20(22:24) rows.

1st pocket opening row (wrong side) Patt 9(11:13), slip next 17 sts onto a holder, patt 17 sts of large pocket lining, patt 11. 37(39:41) sts.

Patt 39(41:43) more rows, so ending with 5th(1st:5th) row of 8th(9th:9th) patt.

Shape armhole

Bind off 5 sts at beg of next row.

Dec row (right side) Patt to last 2 sts, skp.

Cont in patt, dec in this way at end of next 2(3:4) right side rows. 29(30:31) sts.

Patt 14(10:6) rows.

2nd pocket opening row (wrong side) Patt 6(7:8), slip next 15 sts onto a holder, patt 15 sts of small pocket lining, patt 8. 29(30:31) sts.

Patt 10(12:14) rows.

Shape neck

Next row (right side) Patt 6 and leave these 6 sts on a holder for collar, patt to end. 23(24:25) sts.

Dec one st at neck edge on next 8 rows. 15(16:17) sts.

Patt 0(4:8) rows, so ending with a right side row.

Bind off.

collar

Join shoulder seams. With right side facing and size 3 (3¼mm) needles, slip 6 sts from right front holder onto needle, pick up and k 12(16:20) sts up right front neck, 28 sts across back neck, and 12(16:20) sts down left front neck, patt 6 sts from holder. 64(72:80) sts.

1st row (wrong side) Seed st 3, p2, [k2, p2] to last 3 sts, seed st 3.

2nd row Seed st 3, k2, [p2, k2] to last 3 sts, seed st 3.

These 2 rows form rib with seed st at each end. Work until collar measures 4in/10cm, ending with a wrong side row.

Dec one st at each end of next row. Work until collar measures 4in/10cm from dec row. Leave sts on a holder.

armhole edgings

With size 3 (3¼mm) needles, pick up and k 69(77:89) sts around armhole.
Work 4 rows in seed st as for Back.
Bind off knitwise.

lower pocket tops

With size 3 (3¼mm) needles, working across 17 sts on holder, and beg k1,
work 2 rows in seed st.
Buttonhole row (right side) Seed st 8, yo, p2tog, seed st 7.
Work 2 more rows in seed st.
Bind off knitwise.

upper pocket tops

With size 3 (3¼mm) needles, working across 15 sts on holder, and beg p1,
work 2 rows in seed st.
Buttonhole row (right side) Seed st 7, yo, p2tog, seed st 6.
Work 2 rows more in seed st.
Bind off knitwise.

finishing

Ending at dec row of collar, sew in zipper. Fold collar in half onto wrong side
and sew first and last 2 sts to zipper, then each st to corresponding st of pick
up row. Slip stitch pocket linings in place and catch down ends of pocket
tops. Join side and armhole edging seams.

Hattie

An easy-knit scarf with a large pompon at each end, which is the perfect first project for the junior knitter. It is worked in a super-bulky-weight yarn on large needles.

size	5½in x 36in/14cm x 92cm
materials	One 1¾oz/50g ball of Debbie Bliss cashmerino superchunky in Pale Blue (A) and one 1¾oz/50g ball of Debbie Bliss cashmerino aran in Cream (B) Pair of size 11 (U.K. 7½mm) knitting needles
gauge	8 sts and 21 rows to 4in/10cm square over garter st using size 11 (U.K. 7½mm) needles.

abbreviations

cm = centimeters   **k** = knit
in = inches   **st(s)** = stitch(es)

scarf

to make

With size 11 (U.K. 7½mm) needles and A, cast on 17 sts.
Work in garter st (k every row), until scarf measures 36in/92cm.
Bind off.
Make two pompons from B (see page 63), gather the ends of the scarf, and sew pompons in place.

Amy

A classic rib and cable pattern is used in this V-neck cricket-style sweater. It is worked in a cashmere mix that combines the elasticity of wool with the luxury of cashmere.

measurements	To fit ages	4–5	6–7	8–9	years
	Actual measurements				
	Chest	28¾	31½	33¾	in
		73	80	86	cm
	Length	16½	18	19¾	in
		42	46	50	cm
	Sleeve seam	11	12¼	13½	in
	(with cuff turned back)	28	31	34	cm

materials

8(9:10) 1¾oz/50g balls of Debbie Bliss baby cashmerino in Duck Egg (A) and two 1¾oz/50g balls in Ecru (B)
Pair each size 2 and 3 (U.K. 2¾mm and 3¼mm) knitting needles
Size 3 (U.K. 3mm) circular needle
Cable needle

gauge

36 sts and 36 rows to 4in/10cm square over cable patt using size 3 (3¼mm) needles.

abbreviations

alt = alternate
beg = beginning
C6F = slip next 3 sts onto cable needle and hold at front of work, k3, then k3 from cable needle
cm = centimeters

cont = continue
dec = decreas(e)ing
foll = following
in = inches
inc = increas(e)ing
k = knit
p = purl
patt = pattern

rem = remain(ing)
rep = repeat
skp = slip 1, knit 1, pass slipped stitch over
st(s) = stitch(es)
tbl = through back of loop
tog = together

sweater

back

With size 2 (2¾mm) needles and B, cast on 134(146:158) sts.

1st rib row (wrong side) P2, [k2, p2] to end.

2nd rib row K2, [p2, k2] to end.

Rep these 2 rows once more.

Change to A and work 2 rows in rib as set.

Change to B and cont in rib for a further 11 rows.

Change to size 3 (3¼mm) needles and A.

1st row (right side) K2, [p2, k6, p2, k2] to end.

2nd row P2, [k2, p6, k2, p2] to end.

3rd and 4th rows As 1st and 2nd rows.

5th row K2, [p2, C6F, p2, k2] to end.

6th row As 2nd row.

These 6 rows form the patt and are repeated.

Cont in patt until Back measures 14½(16¼:17¾)in/37(41:45)cm from beg, ending with a wrong side row.

Shape neck

Next row Patt 51(55:59), turn, and cont on these sts only, leave rem sts on a spare needle.

Bind off 3 sts at beg of next row and 5 foll alt rows. 33(37:41) sts.

Work even in patt for 4 rows.

Bind off for shoulder.

With right side facing, slip center 32(36:40) sts onto a holder, rejoin yarn to rem sts on spare needle and patt to end. Complete to match first side.

front

Work as given for Back, until Front measures 8¼(9:9¾)in/21(23:25)cm from beg, ending with a wrong side row.

Shape neck

Next row Patt 66(72:78), turn and work on these sts only, leave rem sts on a spare needle.

Dec one st at neck edge on every alt row until 33(37:41) sts rem.

Work even in patt until Front measures same as Back to shoulder bound-off edge, ending with a wrong side row.

Bind off.

With right side facing, slip center 2 sts onto a safety pin, rejoin yarn to rem sts on spare needle, patt to end.

Complete to match first side, reversing shapings.

sleeves

With size 2 (2¾mm) needles and B, cast on 46(50:54) sts.

Beg with a 2nd(1st:2nd) rib row, work 4 rows in rib as for Back.

Change to A and rib 2 rows.

Change to B and rib 27 rows.

Change to size 3 (3¼mm) needles and A.

1st row (right side) P0(0:2), k0(2:2), [p2, k6, p2, k2] to last 10(12:14) sts, p2, k6, p2, k0(2:2), p0(0:2).

2nd row K0(0:2), p0(2:2), [k2, p6, k2, p2] to last 10(12:14) sts, k2, p6, k2, p0(2:2), k0(0:2).

These 2 rows set the position of the patt. Cont in patt as set, inc one st at each end of next row and every foll alt row until there are 116(122:126) sts, working inc sts into patt.

Work even until sleeve measures 13(14¼:15½)in/33(36:39)cm from beg, ending with a wrong side row. Bind off.

neckband

Join right shoulder seam. With right side facing, size 3 (3mm) circular needle and A, pick up and k 71(75:79) sts down left front neck, k 2 sts from safety pin (mark these 2 sts), pick up and k 70(74:78) sts up right front neck, 18 sts down right back neck, k across 32(36:40) sts at center back and dec 4 sts evenly, then pick up and k 19 sts up left back neck. 208(220:232) sts. Work backward and forward in rows.

Change to B.

1st row [p2, k2] to 3 sts before center front marked sts, p1, p2tog tbl, p2, p2tog, p1, [k2, p2] to end.

2nd row [K2, p2] to 2 sts before marked sts, k2tog, k2, skp, [p2, k2] to end.

Working in rib as set and dec 2 sts at center front as before, work 9 rows in B, 2 rows in A and 4 rows in B.

Next row Rib to 2 sts before marked sts, dec 2 sts at center, rib to last 66 sts, [k2, p2, k1, skp, k2tog, k1, p2, k2, p2] 4 times, k2.

Rib 3 rows as now set, dec 2 sts at center front as before.

Change to size 2 (2¾mm) needles.

Next row Rib to 2 sts before marked sts, dec 2 sts at center, rib to last 58 sts, [k2, p2, skp, k2tog, p2, k2, p2] 4 times, k2. 148(160:172) sts.

Cont in rib as set dec 2 sts at center front as before, work 3 rows in B, 2 rows in A and 4 rows in B.

Bind off in rib and dec at center as before.

finishing

Join left shoulder and neckband seam. Matching center of bound-off edge of sleeve to shoulder seam, sew on sleeves. Join side and sleeve seams, reversing seams on lower 2in/5cm for cuff.

Theresa

Here is a wrap-around cardigan with a pretty ruffle edging and ribbon tie. It is knitted in a soft cotton and cashmere mix.

measurements		3–5	5–7	7–9	
	To fit	3–5	5–7	7–9	years
	Actual measurements				
	Chest	27½	29½	31½	in
		70	75	80	cm
	Length to shoulder	11½	12½	13¾	in
		29	32	35	cm
	Sleeve length	9½	10¾	12	in
		24	27	30	cm

materials

5(6:7) 1¾oz/50g balls of Debbie Bliss cotton cashmere in Pale Blue
Pair each size 3 and 5 (U.K. 3¼mm and 3¾mm) knitting needles
Size 6 (U.K. 4mm) circular needle
1yd/1m narrow ribbon

gauge

22 sts and 30 rows to 4in/10cm square over St st using size 5 (3¾mm) needles

abbreviations

beg = beginning
cm = centimeters
cont = continue
foll = following
in = inches
inc = increas(e)ing
k = knit

M1 = make one by picking up the loop lying between st just worked and next st and working into the back of it
p = purl

rem = remain(ing)
rep = repeat
skp = slip 1, knit 1, pass slipped stitch over
st(s) = stitch(es)
St st = stockinette stitch
tog = together

cardigan

back

With size 3 (3¼mm) needles, cast on 79(85:91) sts.

K 3 rows.

Change to size 5 (3¾mm) needles.

Beg with a k row, work 84(92:102) rows in St st.

Shape shoulders

Bind off 10(11:12) sts at beg of next 4 rows.

Bind off rem 39(41:43) sts.

right front	With size 3 (3¼mm) needles, cast on 50(55:60) sts.

With size 3 (3¼mm) needles, cast on 50(55:60) sts.

K 3 rows.

Change to size 5 (3¾mm) needles.

Beg with a k row, work 26(28:32) rows in St st.

Shape neck

1st row (right side) Bind off 6 sts, k to end.

2nd row P to end.

3rd row Bind off 4 sts, k to end.

4th row P to end.

5th row Bind off 2 sts, k to end.

6th row P to end.

7th row K1, skp, k to end.

8th row P to end.

Rep the last 2 rows until 20(22:24) sts rem, ending with a p row.

Work even for 17 rows.

Shape shoulder

Bind off 10(11:12) sts at beg of next row.

Work 1 row.

Bind off rem 10(11:12) sts.

left front

With size 3 (3¼mm) needles, cast on 50(55:60) sts.

K 3 rows.

Change to size 5 (3¾mm) needles.

Beg with a k row, work 27(29:33) rows in St st.

Shape neck

1st row (wrong side) Bind off 6 sts, p to end.

2nd row K to end.

3rd row Bind off 4 sts, p to end.

4th row K to end.

5th row Bind off 2 sts, p to end.

6th row K to last 3 sts, k2tog, k1.

7th row P to end.

Rep the last 2 rows until 20(22:24) sts rem, ending with a p row.

Work even for 16 rows.

Shape shoulder

Bind off 10(11:12) sts at beg of next row.

Work 1 row.

Bind off rem 10(11:12) sts.

sleeves

With size 3 (3¼mm) needles, cast on 40(44:48) sts.
K 3 rows.
Change to size 5 (3¾mm) needles.
Beg with a k row, work in St st and inc one st at each end of the 3rd and every foll 8th row until there are 56(62:68) sts.
Work even until sleeve measures 9½(10¾:12)in/24(27:30)cm from cast-on edge, ending with a wrong side row.
Bind off.

edgings

With right side facing and size 3 (3¼mm) needles, pick up and k 23(25:28) sts evenly along short straight edge of right front.
K 1 row.
Bind off.
Work left front edging in same way.

neck ruffle

Join shoulder seams.
With right side facing and size 6 (4mm) circular needle, beg at bound-off edge of right front edging, pick up and k 70(76:82) sts evenly along right front neck edge, 39(41:43) sts across back neck, and 70(76:82) sts evenly along left front neck edge, ending at bound-off edge of left front edging. 179(193:207) sts.
Work backward and forward in rows as follows:
1st row K2, p to last 2 sts, k2.
2nd row K to end.
3rd row K2, p to last 2 sts, k2.
4th row K5, * M1, k4; rep from * to last 26(28:30) sts, M1, k to end. 217(234:251) sts.
5th to 7th rows As 1st to 3rd rows.
8th row K6, * M1, k5; rep from * to last 26(28:30) sts, M1, k to end. 255(275:295) sts.
9th row K2, p to last 2 sts, k2.
Bind off.

finishing

Matching center of bound-off edge of sleeve to shoulder, sew on sleeves. Cut ribbon into two pieces, one 4in/10cm longer than the other, and sew the longer tie to left front level with neck shaping, the other in the same position on the right front. Join side and sleeve seams, leaving small opening in right side seam level with neck shaping for left front tie.

Cassie

A coat with a loopy edging on the inside and a blackberry stitch detail on the outside. The seams are also on the outside for a more unusual detailing.

measurements	To fit	5–6	7–8	9–10	11–12	years
	Actual measurements					
	Chest	28½	31½	34½	37¾	in
		72	80	88	96	cm
	Length to shoulder	23½	26	28¾	32	in
		60	66	73	81	cm
	Sleeve length	12¼	13¾	15¼	17	in
		31	35	39	43	cm

materials

13(14:15:17) 1¾oz/50g balls of Debbie Bliss merino aran in Lilac
Pair each size 6 and 8 (U.K. 4mm and 5mm) knitting needles
Two short double-pointed size 6 (4mm) needles

gauge

18 sts and 24 rows to 4in/10cm square over St st using size 8 (5mm) needles.

abbreviations

alt = alternate
beg = beginning
cm = centimeters
cont = continue
dec = decreas(e)ing
foll = following
in = inches
inc = increas(e)ing
k = knit
M1 = make one by picking up the loop lying between st just worked and next st and working into the back of it

make loop = k1, leaving st on left-hand needle, bring yarn to front of work between needles, wrap yarn twice around thumb of left hand and take yarn back to wrong side of work between needles, k same st on left-hand needle again and slip it off left needle, let loops slip off thumb, bring yarn to front of work between needles then take it over right needle to make one st, now pass 2 sts on right needle over made st and off needle, loop completed
p = purl
patt = pattern
rem = remain(ing)
rep = repeat
skp = slip 1, knit 1, pass slipped stitch over
st(s) = stitch(es)
St st = stockinette stitch
tog = together

coat

note

● This garment has been designed to be reversible and has been photographed with the seams on the outside. See note on seams in the finishing section at the end of these instructions.

back

With size 8 (5mm) needles, cast on 68(74:82:88) sts.
Beg with a k row, work in St st.
Work 8 rows.
Dec row K6, skp, k to last 8 sts, k2tog, k6.
Work 7(9:11:13) rows.
Rep the last 8(10:12:14) rows 4 times more and the dec row again. 56(62:70:76) sts.
Work even until Back measures 12(12½:13¾:15)in/30(32:35:38)cm from cast-on edge, ending with a p row.
Inc row K2, M1, k to last 2 sts, M1, k2.
Work 5(5:7:7) rows.
Rep the last 6(6:8:8) rows 4 times more and the inc row again. 68(74:82:88) sts.
Work even until Back measures 18(19¾:21¾:24)in/46(50:55:61)cm from cast-on edge, ending with a p row.
Shape armholes
Bind off 5(6:6:7) sts at beg of next 2 rows. 58(62:70:74) sts.
Dec one st at each end of the next and 2(2:3:3) foll alt rows. 52(56:62:66) sts.
Work even until Back measures 23½(26:28¾:32)in/60(66:73:81)cm from cast-on edge, ending with a wrong side row.
Shape shoulders
Bind off 6(7:8:9) sts at beg of next 4 rows.
Bind off rem 28(28:30:30) sts.

left front

With size 8 (5mm) needles, cast on 38(41:45:48) sts.
1st row (right side) K to last 8 sts, then with short size 6 (4mm) needle, [make loop, k1] 4 times.
2nd row With short size 6 (4mm) needle k8, with size 8 (5mm) needle, p to end.
3rd row With size 8 (5mm) needle, k to last 9 sts, with short size 6 (4mm) needle, [make loop, k1] 4 times, k1.
4th row With short size 6 (4mm) needle k8, with size 8 (5mm) needle, p to end.

These 4 rows set the patt and are repeated, using the size 8 (5mm) needles for the St st and size 6 (4mm) needles for loop st edging.

Work 4 rows.

Dec row K6, skp, k to last 8 sts, patt 8.

Work 7(9:11:13) rows.

Rep the last 8(10:12:14) rows 4 times more and the dec row again. 32(35:39:42) sts.

Work even until front measures 12(12½:13¾:15)in/30(32:35:38)cm from cast-on edge, ending with a wrong side row.

Inc row K2, M1, k to last 8 sts, patt 8.

Work 5(5:7:7) rows.

Rep the last 6(6:8:8) rows 4 times more and the inc row again. 38(41:45:48) sts.

Work even until Front measures 18(19¾:21¾:24)in/46(50:55:61)cm from cast-on edge, ending with a wrong side row.

Shape armhole

Bind off 5(6:6:7) sts at beg of next row. 33(35:39:41) sts.

Work 1 row.

Dec one st at armhole edge of the next and 2(2:3:3) foll alt rows. 30(32:35:37) sts.

Work 1 row.

Next row K to last 10 sts, k2tog, patt 8.

Next row Patt to end.

Rep the last 2 rows until 20(22:24:26) sts rem.

Work even until Front measures same as Back to shoulder shaping, ending at armhole edge.

Shape shoulder

Bind off 6(7:8:9) sts at beg of next and foll alt row. 8 sts.

Next row (wrong side) K to last st, inc in last st. 9 sts.

Cont in loop st patt on rem 9 sts until edging fits halfway across back neck. Bind off.

right front

With size 8 (5mm) needles, cast on 38(41:45:48) sts.

1st row (right side) With short size 6 (4mm) needle, [k1, make loop] 4 times, with size 8 (5mm) needle, k to end.

2nd row With size 8 (5mm) needle, p to last 8 sts, with short size 6 (4mm) needle, k8.

3rd row With short size 6 (4mm) needle k1, [k1, make loop] 4 times, with size 8 (5mm) needle, k to end.

4th row With size 8 (5mm) needle, p to last 8 sts, with short size 6 (4mm) needle, k8.

These 4 rows set the patt and are repeated, using the size 8 (5mm) needles for the St st and size 6 (4mm) needles for loop st edging.

Work 4 rows.

Dec row Patt 8, k to last 8 sts, k2tog, k6.

Work 7(9:11:13) rows.

Rep the last 8(10:12:14) rows 4 times more and the dec row again. 32(35:39:42) sts.

Work even until front measures 12(12½:13¾:15)in/30(32:35:38)cm from cast-on edge, ending with a wrong side row.

Inc row Patt 8, k to last 2 sts, M1, k2.

Work 5(5:7:7) rows.

Rep the last 6(6:8:8) rows 4 times more and the inc row again. 38(41:45:48) sts.

Work even until Front measures 18(19¾:21¾:24)in/46(50:55:61)cm from cast-on edge, ending with a right side row.

Shape armhole

Bind off 5(6:6:7) sts at beg of next row. 33(35:39:41) sts.

Dec one st at armhole edge of the next and 2(2:3:3) foll alt rows. 30(32:35:37) sts.

Work 1 row.

Next row Patt 8, skp, k end.

Next row Patt to end.

Rep the last 2 rows until 20(22:24:26) sts rem.

Work even until Front measures same as Back to shoulder shaping, ending at armhole edge.

Shape shoulder

Bind off 6(7:8:9) sts at beg of next and foll alt row. 8 sts.

Next row (right side) Inc in first st, patt to end. 9 sts.

Cont in loop st patt on rem 9 sts, until edging fits halfway across back neck. Bind off.

sleeves

With US 6 (4mm) needles, cast on 34(36:40:44) sts.

K 1 row.

1st row (right side) K2, * make loop, k1; rep from * to end.

2nd row K to end.

3rd row K1, * make loop, k1; rep from * to last st, k1.

4th row K to end.

Rep the last 4 rows once more.

Change to size 8 (5mm) needles.

Beg with a k row, work in St st.

Inc one st at each end of the 3rd and every foll 4th row until there are 64(72:80:88) sts.

Work even until sleeve measures 12¼(13¾:15¼:17)in/31(35:39:43)cm from cast-on edge, ending with a p row.

Shape sleeve top

Bind off 5(6:6:7) sts at beg of next 2 rows. 54(60:68:74) sts.

Dec one st at each end of the next and 2(2:3:3) foll alt rows. 48(54:60:66) sts.

Bind off.

finishing

When sewing together the garment to be reversible, make sure all seams are neatly stitched and yarn ends carefully darned in or they will show. Join shoulder seams. Join bound-off edges of loop edging. Sew row ends to bound-off sts at back neck. With center of bound-off edge of sleeve to shoulder seam, sew sleeves into armholes. Join side and sleeve seams.

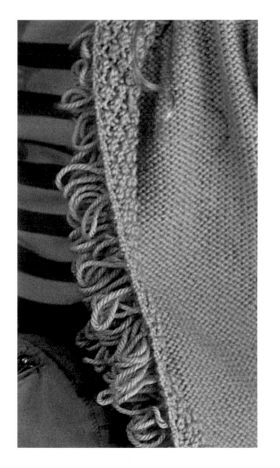

cozy

Striped leg and hand warmers are good projects to start with if you are unsure about tackling complicated colorwork such as Fair Isle or intarsia. They are simple-to-make tubes in colorful stripes.

size
One size to fit ages: 5–10 years

materials
One 1¾oz/50g ball each of Debbie Bliss baby cashmerino in Duck Egg (A), Pale Blue (B), Apple Green (C), Old Rose (D), Pale Pink (E), and Fuchsia (F)
Pair each size 2 and 3 (U.K. 2¾mm and 3¼mm) knitting needles

gauge
44 sts and 33 rows to 4in/10cm square over rib patt without stretching using size 3 (3¼mm) needles.

abbreviations

cm = centimeters	**k** = knit	**rep** = repeat
cont = continue	**p** = purl	**st(s)** = stitch(es)
in = inches	**patt** = pattern	

leg warmers

With size 2 (2¾mm) needles and A, cast on 72 sts.
Work in stripes of 4 rows each of A, B, C, D, E, and F in rib patt as follows:
1st row (right side) P2, * k3, p2; rep from * to end.
2nd row K2, * p3, k2; rep from * to end.
Work a further 22 rows in patt.
Change to size 3 (3¼mm) needles.
Work a further 72 rows.
Change to size 2 (2¾mm) needles.
Work a further 24 rows.
Bind off in rib.
Join seam, matching stripes.

hand warmers

With size 3 (3¼mm) needles and A, cast on 42 sts and work 4 rows in rib as follows:

1st row (right side) P2, * k3, p2; rep from * to end.

2nd row K2, * p3, k2; rep from * to end.

Cont in rib and work in 2 row stripes of B, C, D, E, F, and A.

Work a further 21 rows in patt, so ending with a 1st row in F.

Thumb opening

Next row (wrong side) With F, patt 17, bind off 8, patt to end.

Next row With A, patt 17, cast on 8, patt to end.

Work a further 11 rows in patt.

Work 4 rows using A.

Bind off in rib.

Join seam, matching stripes.

Bill

Multicolored stripes for this sporty hooded top. It knits up quickly in a soft but hardwearing cotton.

measurements

To fit ages	4–6	6–8	8–10	years
Actual measurements				
Chest	31½	35½	39½	in
	80	90	100	cm
Length to shoulder	17	18	19¾	in
	43	46	50	cm
Sleeve length	11	13	15	in
	28	33	38	cm

materials

3(3:4) 1¾oz/50g balls of Debbie Bliss cotton double knitting in Chocolate, and 2(2:3) 1¾oz/50g balls each in Stone, Olive, Willow, Navy, Mid Blue, Burnt Orange, and Bright Pink
Pair each size 3 and 6 (U.K. 3¼mm and 4mm) knitting needles

gauge

20 sts and 28 rows to 4in/10cm square over St st using size 6 (4mm) needles.

abbreviations

alt = alternate
beg = beginning
cm = centimeters
cont = continue
foll = following
in = inches
inc = increase(e)ing

k = knit
M1 = make one by picking up the loop lying between st just worked and next st and working into the back of it

p = purl
patt = pattern
rem = remain(ing)
rep = repeat
st(s) = stitch(es)
St st = stockinette stitch

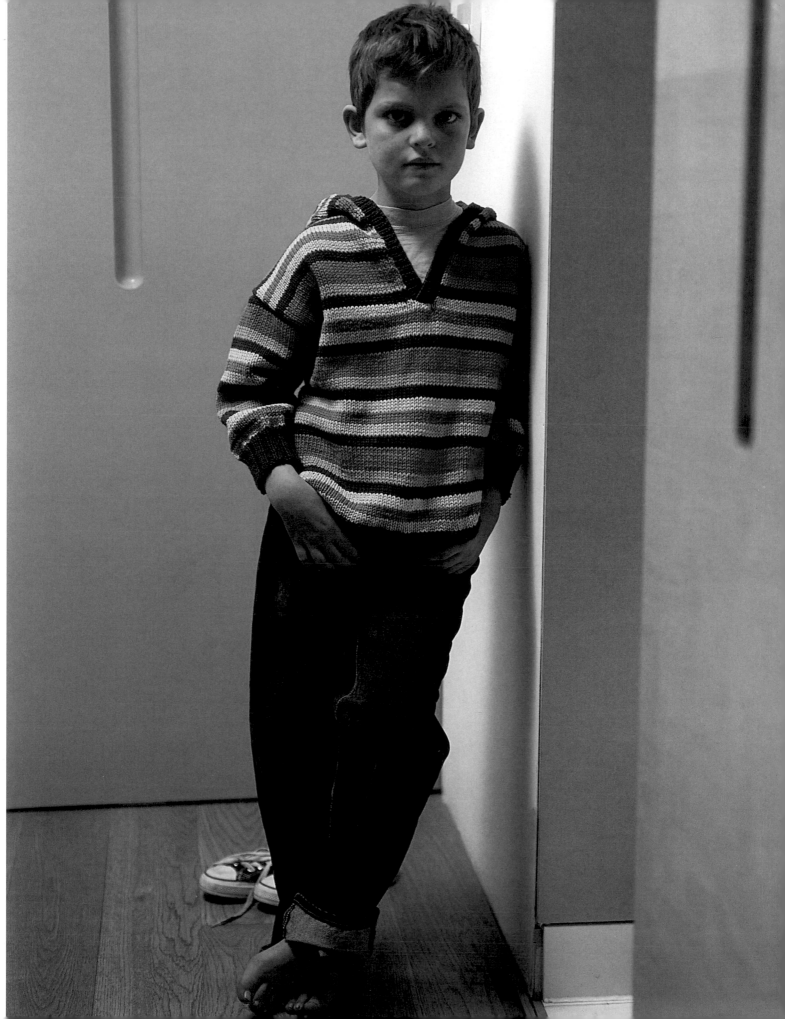

hooded top

note

● Stripe patt: 4 rows each in Stone, Olive, Willow, Navy, Mid Blue, Burnt Orange, Bright Pink, and Chocolate. Rep these 32 rows throughout.

back

With size 3 (3¼mm) needles and Chocolate, cast on 82(90:102) sts.

1st rib row K2, * p2, k2; rep from * to end.

2nd rib row P2, * k2, p2; rep from * to end.

Rep the last 2 rows once more, increasing 0(2:0) sts evenly across last row. 82(92:102) sts.

Change to size 6 (4mm) needles.

Beg with a k row, work in St st and stripe patt as given in note above beg with 4 rows in Stone, until Back measures 17(18:19¾)in/43(46:50)cm from cast-on edge, ending with a p row.

Shape shoulders

Bind off 13(15:17) sts at beg of next 4 rows.

Bind off rem 30(32:34) sts.

front

Work as given for Back until Front measures 11(12:13)in/28(30:33)cm from cast-on edge, ending with a p row.

Divide for front opening

Next row K39(44:49), turn and work on these sts only for first side of front neck, leave rem sts on a spare needle.

Work even until Front measures the same as Back to shoulder, ending at side edge.

Shape shoulder

Bind off 13(15:17) sts at beg of next row and foll alt row.

Work 1 row.

Leave rem 13(14:15) sts on a holder for hood.

With right side facing, rejoin yarn to rem sts on spare needle, bind off center 4 sts, k to end.

Complete to match first side of neck, reversing shaping.

hood

Join shoulder seams.

With right side facing, size 6 (4mm) needles, and keeping stripe patt correct, k across 13(14:15) sts from right front holder, cast on 34(36:38) sts, k across 13(14:15) sts from left front holder. 60(64:68) sts.

Beg with a p row, work 3 rows in St st.

Inc row (right side) K4, M1, k to last 4 sts, M1, k4.

Work even for 5 rows.

Rep the last 6 rows 10(11:12) times more. 82(88:94) sts.

Bind off.

sleeves

With size 3 (3¼mm) needles and Chocolate, cast on 42(46:50) sts.

Work 1½(2:2)in/4(5:5)cm in rib as given for Back, ending with a right side row.

Inc row (wrong side) Rib 4(6:8), * M1, rib 7; rep from * to last 3(5:7) sts, M1, rib 3(5:7). 48(52:56) sts.

Change to size 6 (4mm) needles.

Beg with a k row and working in stripe patt as before, inc one st at each end of the 3rd and every foll 5th row until there are 72(80:88) sts.

Work even until sleeve measures 11(13:15)in/28(33:38)cm from cast-on edge, ending with a p row.

Bind off.

edgings

With right side facing, size 3 (3¼mm) needles, and Chocolate, pick up and k 94(102:110) sts along right front opening and hood.

Work 5 rows in rib.

Bind off in rib.

Rep for left front opening and hood.

finishing

Matching center of bound-off edge of sleeve to shoulder, sew on sleeves. Join side and sleeve seams. Place lower edge of left front band over lower edge of right front band and sew in place to bound-off sts at center front. Fold cast-off edge of hood in half and join seam. Sew cast-on sts of hood to bound-off edge of back neck.

Peg

A very simple ribbed hat with contrast edge and pompon. Knitted in a cashmere mix, it is soft and cozy

sizes	**To fit ages** 1–2 2–3 years
materials	One 1¾oz/50g ball each of Debbie Bliss cashmerino aran in main color Pale Blue (MC) and in contrasting color Cream (CC) Pair of size 8 (5mm) knitting needles
gauge	18 sts and 24 rows to 4in/10cm square over St st using size 8 (5mm) needles.

abbreviations

cm = centimeters	**k** = knit	**rep** = repeat
cont = continue	**p** = purl	**st(s)** = stitch(es)
in = inches	**rem** = remain(ing)	**tog** = together

hat

to make

With size 8 (5mm) needles and CC, cast on 86(98) sts.
1st rib row K2, * p2, k2; rep from * to end.
2nd rib row P2, * k2, p2; rep from * to end.
These 2 rows set the rib.
Work 12 rows more.
Change to MC.
Cont in rib until hat measures 7(8)in/18(20)cm from cast-on edge, ending with a 2nd rib row.
Shape top
1st row K2, * p2tog, k2; rep from * to end.

2nd row P2, * k1, p2; rep from * to end.

3rd row K2, * p1, k2; rep from * to end.

4th row P2, * k1, p2; rep from * to end.

5th row K2tog, * p1, k2tog; rep from * to end.

6th row P1, * k1, p1; rep from * to end.

7th row K1, * p3tog, k1; rep from * to last 2(0) sts, p1(0), k1(0).

8th row P1, * p2tog; rep from * to end.

Break yarn, thread end through rem 12(13) sts, draw up, and secure.

Join seam.

Make a pompon (see page 63) from CC and sew to top of hat.

ROSY

Here is a ribbed scarf with a bright contrasting lining and secret pockets. The unusual zipper detail keeps it firmly in place!

measurements	Approximately 8¾in x 51in/22cm x 130cm
materials	Four 1¾oz/50g balls each of Debbie Bliss merino dk in Red (A) and Bright Pink (B) Pair of size 6 (4mm) knitting needles 10in/25cm open-ended zipper
gauge	22 sts and 28 rows to 4in/10cm square over St st using size 6 (4mm) needles.

abbreviations

beg = beginning	**in** = inches	**rev St st** = reverse stockinette stitch
cm = centimeters	**k** = knit	**st(s)** = stitch(es)
cont = continue	**p** = purl	**St st** = stockinette stitch

scarf

to make

Outside pocket
With size 6 (4mm) needles and A, cast on 48 sts.
Beg with a k row, work 6in/15cm in St st, ending with a k row.
K 1 row, p 1 row.

Main scarf
With needle holding sts held in left hand, cast on 48 sts in B onto this needle for lining.
Next row (right side) K48 sts in B, k48 sts in A, twisting yarns at color change to link color areas.
Next row P48 in A, p48 in B.
Cont to work St st in this way, linking yarns at color change on every row, until area B measures 51in/130cm, ending with a k row.
Next row (wrong side) Bind off 48 sts in A knitwise, p to end in B. 48 sts.

Lining pocket
Next row (right side) P.
Next row K.
These 2 rows form rev St st and are repeated for 6in/15cm, ending with a k row.
Bind off knitwise.

finishing

Fold pockets up onto right side and slip stitch side edges in place. Fold scarf in half lengthwise and slip stitch cast-on edge of lining to outer scarf and bound-off edge of outer scarf to lining. Using mattress stitch, join outer scarf to lining for 6in/15cm from each end, so ending at top of each pocket. Place markers 10in/25cm above each pocket, join seam in mattress stitch between markers. Hand-stitch zipper in place where the seam has been left open between pockets and markers. Stitch zipper to outer scarf first, then stitch to lining.

Ruby

This brightly colored poncho can be worn as a skirt or in the more conventional way, around the body. Either way, it is a real winter warmer.

measurements	**One size to fit**	7–10	years
	Actual measurements		
	Length	16½	in
		42	cm

materials

Two 1¾oz/50g balls each of Debbie Bliss merino aran in Stone (A), Pale Blue (B), and Indigo (C)

One 1¾oz/50g ball each in Forest (D), Apple Green (E), Mid Blue (F), Ecru (G), Pale Pink (H), Fuchsia (J), and Red (K)

Pair each size 7 and 8 (U.K. 4½mm and 5mm) knitting needles

gauge

18 sts and 24 rows to 4in/10cm square over St st using size 8 (5mm) needles.

abbreviations

beg = beginning
cm = centimeters
cont = continue
dec = decreas(e)ing
in = inches
k = knit

p = purl
patt = pattern
rem = remain(ing)
skp = slip 1, knit 1, pass slipped stitch over

st(s) = stitch(es)
St st = stockinette stitch
tog = together
yo = yarn over

Chart 1

4 sts

Chart 2

6 sts

Chart 3

21 sts

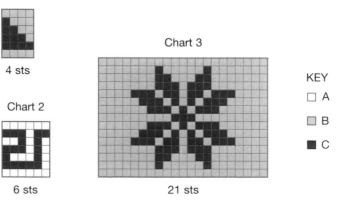

KEY
☐ A
▨ B
■ C

poncho

back and front

(both alike)

With size 7 (4½mm) needles and A, cast on 153 sts.

K 1 row.

Change to size 8 (5mm) needles.

Beg with a k row, work in St st in patt as follows:

1st row (1st row of Chart 1) With B, skp, k to last 2 sts, k2tog. 151 sts.

2nd row (2nd row of Chart 1) With C, p to end.

3rd row (3rd row of Chart 1) With B, skp, with C k3, [k across 4 sts of 3rd row of Chart] 36 times, with B, k2tog. 149 sts.

Dec one st at each end of every right side row, work in patt as follows:

Cont to work rem 3 rows of Chart 1.

Work in St st stripes of 2 rows each of D, E, F, G, H, J, and K. 133 sts.

Work from Chart 2 as follows:

21st row (1st row of Chart 2) With A, skp, k to last 2 sts, k2tog. 131 sts.

22nd row (2nd row of Chart 2) With A, p3, [p across 6 sts of 2nd row of Chart] 21 times, with A, p2.

Dec one st at each end of every right side row, work rem 5 rows of Chart 2 in patt. 125 sts.

Dec one st at each end of every right side row, work in St st stripes of 2 rows each of F, E, G, H, J, and K. 113 sts.

Work from Chart 3 as follows:

40th row (1st row of Chart 3) With B, p to end.

41st row (2nd row of Chart 3) With B, skp, k2, [k across 21 sts of 2nd row of Chart] 5 times, with B k2, k2tog. 111 sts.

Dec one st at each end of every right side row, work rem 13 rows of Chart 3 in patt. 99 sts.

Cont to dec as before and work in St st stripes of 2 rows each of D, E, F, G, H, J, and K. 85 sts.

Work from Chart 2 as follows:

69th row (1st row of Chart 2) With A, skp, k to last 2 sts, k2tog. 83 sts.

70th row (2nd row of Chart 2) With A, p3, [p across 6 sts of 2nd row of Chart] 13 times, with A, p2.

Dec one st at each end of every right side row, work rem 5 rows of Chart 2 in patt. 77 sts.

Dec one st at each end of every right side row, work in St st stripes of 2 rows each of F, E, G, H, J, and K. 65 sts.

88th row (1st row of Chart 1) With B, p to end.

89th row (2nd row of Chart 1) With C, skp, k to last 2 sts, k2tog. 63 sts.

90th row (3rd row of Chart 1) With B, p2, [p across 4 sts of 3rd row of Chart] 15 times, with B, p1.

Dec one st at each end of every right side row, work rem 3 rows of Chart 1 in patt. 59 sts.

Cont to dec as before and work in St st stripes of 2 rows each of D, E, F, G, H, J, and K. 45 sts.

Change to size 7 (4½mm) needles.

Eylet row With A, k3, [k2tog, yo, k7] 4 times, k2tog, yo, k4.

Next row With A, k to end.

With A, bind off.

finishing

Carefully matching patterns, join center front and back seams.

Cord

Cut one 6½yd/6m length in each of the ten colors. Knot the strands together at each end. Hook one end over a door handle and insert a needle through the other end. Twist the needle clockwise until the strands are tightly twisted. Holding the cord in the center with one hand, bring the ends together and let the two halves twist together. Knot the cut ends together to form a tassel and trim. Knot the folded end and cut to form a tassel. Thread through eyelets to tie at center front.

caitlín

A classic denim-jacket-style top with pocket flaps and button tabs. Texture is created with a combination of seed stitch and traveling diagonal cables. It is knitted in the pale blue from my cotton denim aran yarn to create a faded, washed-out look.

measurements

To fit	3–4	5–6	7–8	9–10	years
Actual measurements					
Chest	28¾	30¼	33¾	36	in
	73	77	86	91	cm
Length	11¾	13¾	16	17	in
	30	35	41	43	cm
Sleeve seam	9¾	11	12¼	13¾	in
	25	28	31	35	cm

materials

10(11:12:13) 1¾oz/50g balls of Debbie Bliss denim aran in Pale Blue
Pair of size 7 (U.K. 4½mm) knitting needles
Cable needle
9(10:10:10) buttons

gauges

18 sts and 24 rows over St st and 18 sts and 32 rows over seed st, both to a 4in/10cm square using size 7 (4½mm) needles.

abbreviations

alt = alternate
C6B = slip next 3 sts onto cable needle and hold at back of work, k3, then k3 from cable needle
C6F = slip next 3 sts onto cable needle and hold at front of work, k3, then k3 from cable needle
cm = centimeters
cont = continue

dec = decreas(e)ing
foll = following
in = inches
inc = increas(e)ing
k = knit
kp = knit and purl into next st
M1 = make one by picking up the loop lying between st just worked and next st and working into the back of it

p = purl
patt = pattern
pk = purl and knit into next st
rem = remain(ing)
rep = repeat
st(s) = stitch(es)
St st = stockinette stitch
tog = together
yo = yarn over

jacket

note

● When measuring the length of garment pieces, take the measurements on the seed st sections, not the stockinette stitch.

back

With size 7 (4½mm) needles, cast on 57(59:63:65) sts.
Seed st row K1, [p1, k1] to end.
Rep this row 5 more times.
Inc row (right side) Seed st 13(13:15:15) sts, p1, k2, M1, k3, p1, k17(19:19:21), p1, k3, M1, k2, p1, seed st 13(13:15:15). 59(61:65:67) sts.
Now work in patt as follows:
1st row (wrong side) Seed st 13(13:15:15) sts, k1, p6, k1, p17(19:19:21), k1, p6, k1, seed st 13(13:15:15).
2nd row Seed st 13(13:15:15) sts, p1, k6, p1, k17(19:19:21), p1, k6, p1, seed st 13(13:15:15).
3rd row As 1st row.
4th row Seed st 13(13:15:15) sts, p1, C6B, p1, M1, k17(19:19:21), M1, p1, C6F, p1, seed st 13(13:15:15). 61(63:67:69) sts.
5th row Seed st 13(13:15:15) sts, k1, p6, k1, p19(21:21:23), k1, p6, k1, seed st 13(13:15:15).
6th row Seed st 13(13:15:15) sts, p1, k6, p1, k19(21:21:23), p1, k6, p1, seed st 13(13:15:15).
These 6 rows set the position of the patt.
Cont in patt, working cable and 2 inc sts on next 4th and 6(7:9:10) foll 6th rows, taking all inc sts into center St st panel. 75(79:87:91) sts.
After last cable and inc row, work 5 rows in patt as set.
Shape armholes
Next row (right side) Bind off 5 sts, with one st on needle, seed st next 7(7:9:9), p1, C6B, p1, M1, k33(37:41:45), M1, p1, C6F, p1, seed st to end.
Next row Bind off 5 sts, patt to end. 67(71:79:83) sts.
Next row Seed st 8(8:10:10), p1, k6, p1, seed st 35(39:43:47), p1, k6, p1, seed st 8(8:10:10).
Next row Seed st 8(8:10:10), k1, p6, k1, seed st 35(39:43:47), k1, p6, k1, seed st 8(8:10:10).
Rep the last 2 rows once more.
Next row Seed st 7(7:9:9), p2tog, C6B, p1, M1, seed st 35(39:43:47), M1, p1, C6F, p2tog, seed st 7(7:9:9).
Cont in patt as now set, dec one st at outer edge of each cable and inc one st

at inner edge of each cable on every foll 6th row, so keeping armhole edge straight and moving cables toward armhole, working all inc sts into center seed st panel, until a total of 15(17:21:22) cable twists have been worked, then work a further 1(5:1:3) rows after last cable row.

Shape shoulders

Bind off 23(25:28:29) sts at beg of next 2 rows, working 2 sts tog in center of each cable.

Leave rem 21(21:23:25) sts on a holder.

pocket linings
(make 2)

With size 7 (4½mm) needles, cast on 13(15:17:19) sts.

Beg with a k row, work 14(16:18:20) rows in St st.

Leave sts on a spare needle.

pocket flaps
(make 2)

With size 7 (4½mm) needles, cast on 5(7:5:7) sts.

1st row (right side) K1, [p1, k1] to end.

2nd row Pk, [p1, k1] to last 2 sts, p1, kp. 7(9:7:9) sts.

3rd row (make buttonhole) P1, k1, p0(1:0:1), p(k:p:k)2tog, yo, k0(1:0:1), p1, k1, p1.

4th row Kp, [k1, p1] to last 2 sts, k1, pk.

5th row As 1st row.

6th row As 2nd row.

7th row P1, [k1, p1] to end.

8th row As 4th row.

9th row As 1st row.

10th row As 2nd row. 15(17:15:17) sts.

3rd and 4th sizes only

11th row As 7th row.

12th row As 4th row.

13th row As 1st row.

14th row As 2nd row.

All sizes

Leave these 15(17:19:21) sts on a spare needle.

left front

With size 7 (4½mm) needles, cast on 38(40:42:44) sts.

1st row (right side) [P1, k1] to end.

2nd row [K1, p1] to end.

3rd row P1, k1, yo, k2tog, [p1, k1] to end.

4th row As 2nd row.

5th row As 1st row.

6th row As 2nd row.

Next row (right side) Bind off 7(8:8:9), with one st on needle, seed st next 12(12:14:14), p1, k2, M1, k3, p1, k6(7:7:8), seed st 5 as set. 32(33:35:36) sts.

Now work in patt as follows:

1st row (wrong side) Seed st 5, p6(7:7:8), k1, p6, k1, seed st 13(13:15:15).

2nd row Seed st 13(13:15:15), p1, k6, p1, k6(7:7:8), seed st 5.

3rd row As 1st row.

4th row Seed st 13(13:15:15), p1, C6B, p1, M1, k6(7:7:8), seed st 5. 33(34:36:38) sts.

5th row Seed st 5, p7(8:8:9), k1, p6, k1, seed st 13(13:15:15).

6th row Seed st 13(13:15:15), p1, k6, p1, k7(8:8:9), seed st 5.

These 6 rows set the position of the patt, with 5 seed sts at front edge for buttonband, and 13(13:15:15) seed st at side edge, worked on every row. Cont in patt, working cable and one inc st on next 4th and 6(7:9:10) foll 6th rows, taking all inc sts into St st panel. 40(42:46:48) sts.

After last cable and inc row, work 5 rows in patt as set.

Shape armhole

Next row (right side) Bind off 5 sts, with one st on needle, seed st next 7(7:9:9) sts, p1, C6B, p1, M1, k to last 5 sts, seed st 5. 36(38:42:44) sts.

Next row Seed st 5, p1, bind off next 13(15:17:19) sts knitwise, k1, p6, k1, seed st to end.

Place pocket lining and flap

Next row (right side) Seed st 8(8:10:10), p1, k6, p1, with needle holding pocket flap sts in front of work, p tog first st of flap with one st of body, then with needle holding pocket lining sts to the back of the work, seed st tog all pocket lining sts with next 13(15:17:19) sts of flap, then p tog last st of flap with next st of body, seed st 5.

Next row Seed st 20(22:24:26), k1, p6, k1, seed st to end.

Next row Seed st 8(8:10:10), p1, k6, p1, seed st to end.

Next row Seed st 20(22:24:26), k1, p6, k1, seed st to end.

Next row Seed st 7(7:9:9), p2tog, C6B, p1, M1, seed st to end.

Cont in this way, working one dec st at outer edge of cable and one inc st at inner edge of cable, on every foll 6th row until a total of 12(15:18:19) cable twists have been worked. Patt a further 2(2:4:4) rows after last cable row, so ending at front edge.

Shape neck

Keeping patt correct, cont to work the cable and the inc and dec sts on every 6th row as before, bind off at beg (neck edge) of next and every foll alt row, 4 sts once, 3 sts once, 2 sts 2(2:3:3) times, and one st 2(2:1:2) times. 23(25:28:29) sts.

Work 6(4:4:4) rows more in patt.

Bind off in patt working 2 sts tog in center of cable.

right front
With size 7 (4½mm) needles, cast on 38(40:42:44) sts.

1st row (right side) [K1, p1] to end.

2nd row [P1, k1] to end.

3rd row [K1, p1] to last 4 sts, k2tog, yo, k1, p1.

4th row As 2nd row.

5th row K1, p1, yo, p2tog, [k1, p1] to end.

6th row Bind off 7(8:8:9), seed st to end.

Next row (right side) Seed st 5, k6(7:7:8), p1, k3, M1, k2, p1, seed st 13(13:15:15) as set. 32(33:35:36) sts.

Now work in patt as follows:

1st row (wrong side) Seed st 13(13:15:15), k1, p6, k1, p6(7:7:8), seed st 5.

2nd row Seed st 5, k6(7:7:8), p1, k6, p1, seed st 13(13:15:15).

3rd row As 1st row.

4th row Seed st 5, k6(7:7:8), M1, p1, C6F, p1, seed st 13(13:15:15).

5th row Seed st 13(13:15:15), k1, p6, k1, p7(8:8:9), seed st 5.

6th row Seed st 5, k7(8:8:9), p1, k6, p1, seed st 13(13:15:15).

These 6 rows set the position of the patt, with 5 seed sts at front edge for buttonhole band, and 13(13:15:15) seed st at side edge, worked on every row. Cont in patt, working cable and one inc st on next 4th and every foll 6th row, taking inc sts into St st panel and working buttonholes as set on next 10th(10th:14th:12th) and 3(4:4:4) foll 18th(18th:22nd:24th) rows.

Work as for Left Front, reversing all shapings and continuing to work buttonholes as directed, binding off pocket sts on same wrong side row as armhole bind-off and working pocket lining and flap placement on foll row. When final buttonhole has been worked, patt a further 3 rows, then shape neck.

sleeves
With size 7 (4½mm) needles, cast on 35(39:43:47) sts.

Work 6 rows in seed st as given for Back.

Inc row (right side) Seed st 9(11:11:13), p1, k3, M1, k2, p1, k3(3:7:7), p1, k2, M1, k3, p1, seed st 9(11:11:13). 37(41:45:49) sts.

1st row Seed st 9(11:11:13), k1, p6, k1, p3(3:7:7), k1, p6, k1, seed st 9(11:11:13).

2nd row Seed st 9(11:11:13), p1, k6, p1, k3(3:7:7), p1, k6, p1, seed st 9(11:11:13).

3rd row As 1st row.

4th row Seed st 9(11:11:13), p1, C6B, p1, M1, k3(3:7:7), M1, p1, C6F, p1, seed st 9(11:11:13).

5th row Seed st 9(11:11:13), k1, p6, k1, p5(5:9:9), k1, p6, k1, seed st 9(11:11:13).

6th row Seed st 9(11:11:13), p1, k6, p1, k5(5:9:9), p1, k6, p1, seed st 9(11:11:13).

These 6 rows set the position of the patt.

Cont in patt, working cables and inc sts on next 4th and every foll 6th row, until there are 61(67:75:79) sts, taking all inc sts into center St st panel. Work until sleeve measures 9¾(11:12¼:13¾)in/25(28:31:35)cm from beg, ending with a right side row. Mark each end of last row and work a further 8 rows but do not work any inc sts on these 8 rows.

collar

Join shoulder seams. With right side facing and size 7 (4½mm) needles, beg 4 sts in from right front edge, pick up and k 20 sts up right front neck, seed st across 21(21:23:25) sts on back neck holder, pick up and k 20 sts down left front neck ending 4 sts in from front edge. 61(61:63:65) sts. Work 2¼in/6cm in seed st as set by back neck sts. Bind off in seed st.

finishing

Matching center of bound-off edge of sleeve to shoulder, sew sleeves into armholes, easing to fit, with row ends above markers sewn to bound-off sts at underarm. Join sleeve seams. Join side seams with back seed st lower band, sewn behind side buttonhole extensions. Sew buttons onto back band, front band and pockets to match buttonholes.

Bug

Here is the snuggest of snug hats in the Inca style, with earflaps in gray and bright stripes.

size	One size to fit 4 years and upward
materials	One 1¾oz/50g ball each of Debbie Bliss merino aran in Pink (A), Red (B), and Grey (C) Pair of size 8 (5mm) knitting needles
gauge	18 sts and 24 rows to 4in/10cm square over St st using size 8 (5mm) needles.

abbreviations

beg = beginning
dec = decreas(e)ing
in = inches
inc = increas(e)ing
k = knit
M1 = make one by picking up the loop lying between st just worked and next st and working into the back of it
p = purl
rem = remain(ing)
s2kp = slip 2, k1, pass 2 slipped sts over
st(s) = stitch(es)
St st = stockinette stitch
tog = together

hat

earflaps (make 2)

With size 8 (5mm) needles and A, cast on 11 sts.
Inc row (right side) K1, M1, k to last st, M1, k1.
P 1 row.
Work inc row once more. 15 sts.
Beg with a p row, work 9 rows in St st.
Leave sts on a holder.

main hat

With size 8 (5mm) needles and B, cast on 15 sts, cut yarn and leave sts on needle.

Cast on 43 sts onto same needle, cut yarn, and leave sts on needle. Cast on 15 sts onto same needle, do not cut yarn.

Next row (right side) With B, k first 15 sts on needle, k across 15 sts of first earflap, k next 43 sts on needle, k across 15 sts of second earflap, k rem 15 sts on needle. 103 sts.

Beg with a p row, work 27 rows in St st in stripes as follows: 11 rows B, 6 rows C, 4 rows A, 2 rows C, 4 rows B.

Shape top

1st dec row (right side) With B, k5, s2kp, [k7, s2kp] 9 times, k5. 83 sts.

Beg with a p row, work in St st in stripes as follows: 3 rows B, 2 rows A, 4 rows C.

2nd dec row (right side) With B, k1, k2tog, [k7, s2kp] 7 times, k7, skp, k1. 67 sts.

Beg with a p row, work 5 more rows in B.

3rd dec row (right side) With B, k1, k2tog, [k5, s2kp] 7 times, k5, skp, k1. 51 sts.

P 1 row in B.

4th dec row (right side) With B, k1, k2tog, [k5, s2kp] 5 times, k5, skp, k1. 39 sts.

Work 1 row in B, then 2 rows in A.

5th dec row (right side) With A, k1, k2tog, [k3, s2kp] 5 times, k3, skp, k1. 27 sts.

Work 3 rows in A.

6th dec row (right side) With A, k1, k2tog, [k1, s2kp] 5 times, k1, skp, k1. 15 sts.

Work 1 row in A, then 2 rows in B.

7th dec row (right side) With B, k1, [k2tog] 7 times. 8 sts.

P 1 row in B.

8th dec row (right side) With B, [k2tog] 4 times. 4 sts.

Leaving a long end, break yarn, thread through sts, draw up, and secure.

edgings

With right side facing, size 7 (4½mm) needles and C, pick up and k 15 sts across back edge, 30 sts around first earflap, 43 sts across front edge, 30 sts around second earflap, and 15 sts across back edge. 133 sts.

Bind off knitwise.

finishing

Join back seam, matching stripes.

suppliers

For suppliers of Debbie Bliss yarns please contact:

U.S.A.
Knitting Fever Inc.,
35 Debevoise Avenue
Roosevelt, New York 11575
Tel: (516) 546-3600
Fax: (516) 546-6871
E-mail: knittingfever@knittingfever.com
Web site: www.knittingfever.com

Canada
Diamond Yarns Ltd.,
155 Martin Ross Avenue, Unit 3, Toronto,
Ontario M3J 2L9
Tel: 001 416 736 6111
Web site: www.diamondyarn.com

U.K.
Designer Yarns Ltd.,
Units 8–10 Newbridge Industrial Estate,
Pitt Street, Keighley,
West Yorkshire BD21 4PQ, England
Tel: +44 (0)1535 664222
Fax: +44 (0)1535 664333
Web site: www.designeryarns.uk.com
E-mail: jane@designeryarns.uk.com

Australia
Sunspun,
185 Canterbury Road,
Canterbury VIC 3126
Tel: +61 (0)3 9830 1609
E-mail: shop@sunspun.com.au
Web site: www.sunspun.com.au

Belgium
Pavan,
Meerlaanstraat 73
9860 Balegem (Oosterzele)
Tel: +32 9 221 85 94
E-mail: pavan@pandora.be

Denmark
Strikkeboden,
Krystalgade 16,
1172 Copenhagen K.
Tel: +45 4583 0127
Email: jens.toersleff@get2net.dk

France
Elle Tricote,
8 Rue de Coq, 67000 Strasbourg
Tel: +33 03 88 230313
Fax: +33 03 88230169
Web site: www.elletricote.com.fr

Germany
Designer Yarns,
Handelsagentur Klaus Koch,
Pontinusweg 7, D-50859 Köln
Tel/Fax: +49 (0)2234 77573
Web site: www.designeryarns.de

Japan
Eisaku Noro & Co Ltd,
55 Shimoda Ohibino Azaichou,
Ichinomita Aichi, 491 0105
Tel: +81 52 203 5100
Fax: +81 52 203 5077

Mexico
Red Color S.A. DE CV.,
San Antonio 105,
Col. Santa Maria,
Monterrey NL 64650
Tel: +52 818 173 3700
Email: Abremer@starsoft.co.mx

Spain
Oyambre,
Paul Claris 145,
08009 Barcelona
Tel/Fax: +34 93487 26272

Sweden
Hamilton Design,
Länggatan 20, SE-64730, Mariefred
Tel: +46 (0)1591 2006
Web site: www.hamiltondesign.biz

acknowledgments

I would like to thank the following for making this book possible:

- The wonderful knitters, Gill Borley, Cynthia Brent, Sally Buss, Pat Church, Penny Hill, Shirley Kennet, Maisie Lawrence, and Frances Wallace.
- Penny Hill, for pattern compiling and coordinating knitters.
- Rosy Tucker, for pattern checking, moral support, and contributing to the designs in the book.
- Sandra Lousada, for the beautiful photography and her invaluable insight and collaboration on all of my projects, and her assistants, Anne and Veronica.
- Julie Mansfield, for the terrific styling and her contribution to the look of the projects.
- Emma Callery, the editor, for being super efficient but also for being brilliant to work with.
- Christine Wood, the designer, for the great design of the book.
- Carey Smith, Fiona MacIntyre, and Grace Cheetham at Ebury, for their commitment to the project.
- Helen Hutton at Ebury, for her calm efficiency.
- Heather Jeeves, my wonderful agent.
- The models, Alexander, Beth, Buddleia, Caitlin, Fela, Max, Milan, Molly, Nell, and Woody.
- The suppliers, distributors, agents, and knitters who support my books and yarns.